Cover to Cover 3

Reading Comprehension and Fluency

Richard R. Day and Leslie Ono

OXFORD

UNIVERSITY PRESS

Contents

Introduction

Cover to Cover 3 is the third in a three-level reading series that helps students become skilled, strategic readers who enjoy reading in English. *Cover to Cover* combines **intensive reading** with **extensive reading,** so your students will learn the strategies necessary for academic work *and* become fluent, confident readers.

What is intensive reading?

Intensive reading focuses on building language awareness and comprehension. It often involves relatively challenging texts, and students encountering some unfamiliar language. Parts 1 and 2 of each unit in *Cover to Cover* focus on intensive reading, and provide students with strategies for dealing with these kinds of texts.

What is extensive reading?

Extensive reading focuses on fluency development and reading for pleasure. Two key principles are (1) students should read as much as possible, and (2) texts should be easy and well within students' linguistic competence. Easy texts mean that students are able to read more and faster, and this kind of practice helps students in many ways: improved reading skills, improved writing skills, increased vocabulary knowledge, and increased motivation. The Extensive Reading section at the end of each unit in *Cover to Cover* provides students with an opportunity to experience this approach.

What is in a unit?

Part 1 and **Part 2** of each unit develop reading strategies such as predicting the topic, skimming for the main idea, scanning, and recognizing points of view. Part 1 focuses mainly on comprehension strategies; Part 2 focuses on developing both fluency and comprehension through activities such as timed reading. The reading passages come from a variety of genres including magazine articles, newspaper articles and web sites.

The **Extensive Reading** section enables students to read for enjoyment and pleasure and continue their fluency development. The reading passages are extracts from the Oxford Bookworms Library collection of graded readers. *Cover to Cover 3* features extracts from stage 3 Bookworms, including popular classics such as *The Picture of Dorian Gray* and *The Wind in the Willows.* The Bookworms extracts are longer than the Part 1 and 2 reading texts, and the language is also graded at a lower level. This enables students to read faster and maintain comprehension. We hope that reading the Bookworms extracts will also motivate students to become enthusiastic, independent readers, who read books from cover to cover.

Unit 1

Beauty

Discuss the questions.

1. Which of the people in the photo do you think are good-looking? Why do you think so?

2. Which physical traits are considered beautiful in your country?

This unit is about current trends in beauty. In Part 1, you will read about male beauty trends. In Part 2, you will read about the growing popularity of plastic surgery. The unit is followed by Extensive Reading 1, which is an extract from a book called *The Picture of Dorian Gray*. It is about a young man, Dorian Gray, who is very concerned with his own beauty.

Before Reading

Discuss the questions.

1. What is a typical morning routine for a man before he goes to work?
2. Do you think men are getting more concerned with the way they look?

Comprehension Strategy: Identifying Supporting Details

Supporting details are used to reinforce or support the main idea of a paragraph. Types of supporting details include verifiable facts, statistics, quotes from experts, opinions of individuals, perceived trends, examples, etc.

A. Scan the text for the details (1–3). Match them with the ideas they support (a–c).

.... 1. David Beckham   **a**. To show the trend includes many different countries.

.... 2. Mr. Beauty   **b**. To show the role of the media.

.... 3. facial masks   **c**. To show the trend is expensive.

B. Read the whole text and answer the questions that follow.

🎧 *CD 1 Track 2*

Male Beauty

1   Seung Lee, age 26, is a manager in a high-end department store in Seoul, Korea. Like many men, he wakes up in the morning, enjoys a cup of coffee, and starts getting ready for work. Unlike most men, Seung's grooming routine can take up to one hour! Seung not only showers and shaves but also carefully sculpts and styles his hair with three different brand-name hair products. He then gently applies several expensive skin moisturizers, and makes sure not to forget the sunblock. Finally, Seung takes his time selecting a hip outfit from his large wardrobe of designer suits, shirts, ties, and shoes.

2   Not only do these preparations cost Seung time, but they also cost him money. Monthly, he spends about 800 dollars on designer clothes, 200 dollars on spa treatments, and 300 dollars for cosmetics, such as hair products, eye creams, and facial masks.

3   Several years ago, Seung's expensive and time-consuming interest in his appearance may have seemed strange. However, recently, the growing trend in male beauty is becoming more mainstream. In fact, men from all different countries are taking a closer look in the mirror. In Western countries, such as the United States and Britain, such

men are sometimes called *metrosexuals*. This term was first used by British journalist Mark Simpson to describe such young men who have a lot of spending money and enjoy the best shopping, gyms, salons, and spas. This trend has also caught on in Asian countries: in Korea these men are referred to as *Mr. Beauty*, and in China they're known as *aimei nanren*, or "love beauty men."

4   Why is male beauty recently becoming so popular? First, the definition of masculinity may be changing. As gender roles[1] are changing, men are less afraid to care about their looks. So, they are spending more time and money on style, grooming, and fashion. Furthermore, consumerism is thriving and statistics show strong economies are allowing for more spending money. As a result, many men are choosing to invest their extra cash in their looks and clothes.

5   The media are also playing a large role in popularizing the male beauty trend while profiting from it too. Recently, there has been a growing selection of health and fashion magazines which are aimed at men. Additionally, television shows which offer makeover advice and fashion tips are now popular with both men and women. Famous media figures, such as David Beckham, the British soccer player, also have a strong impact. Beckham is not only well-known for his soccer skills but also for his cool hairstyles, sarongs, and nail polish.

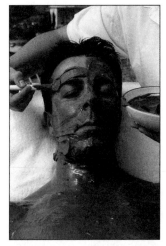

6   This trend can be expensive for men, but the rewards may be worth it. Tatsuo Yamakawa, a 32-year-old businessman from Tokyo, says his careful grooming and concern about fashion have helped him become successful at work. "If we look good on the outside, then we can feel confident on the inside," says Tatsuo. "The people you work with, including your customers, can sense that confidence and will react positively to you. This is an important key to success."

7   Seung says that his fashionable appearance has helped him to meet women. "Women don't want to be with a man who is sloppy," he says. "They like men who are confident, fashionable, and know how to take care of themselves."

8   What do women think about this boom in male beauty? Song Yang, from Beijing, China, likes how her boyfriend is concerned about his appearance. "It's nice to have a boyfriend who enjoys shopping for clothes or a relaxing day at the spa with me," says Song.

9   Despite these good points, however, Song does have one major criticism—"It's difficult to compete with him for time in front of the mirror!"

1 gender roles the different ways men and women are expected to act in society

Checking Comprehension

Answer the questions.

1. What is the main idea of this article?
    a. These days, men have more money.
    b. These days, more men care about their looks.
    c. These days, more men want to look like women.

2. Why does Seung Lee take a long time to get ready in the morning?
    a. He often wakes up late.
    b. He doesn't have enough clothes to choose from.
    c. He is very careful with his grooming and outfit selection.

3. What is one reason that the male beauty trend is popular?
    a. Men are more comfortable caring about their looks.
    b. Men are interested in women who care about their looks.
    c. Consumerism is decreasing.

4. Where is this trend popular?
    a. In Western countries.
    b. In Asian countries.
    c. In different countries all over the world.

5. According to Tatsuo Yamakawa, how can caring about looks help a man?
    a. He can become famous.
    b. He can meet more women.
    c. He can be successful at work.

6. Which statement about the male beauty trend is NOT true?
    a. The media has helped to popularize this trend.
    b. Women like this trend.
    c. It is inexpensive for men.

Looking at Vocabulary in Context

A. Find the words in bold in the text. Circle the word or phrase that has the closest meaning.

1. **Sculpts** (par. 1) means *shapes / cuts*.
2. **Mainstream** (par. 3) means accepted by *most people / very few people*.
3. **Masculinity** (par. 4) means *female / male* characteristics.
4. **Consumerism** (par. 4) means the idea that *buying and selling things / saving money* is important.
5. **Profiting** (par. 5) means *losing / gaining* benefits.
6. **Sloppy** (par. 7) means *messy / neat*.

B. Fill in the blanks with the words in bold from A. Be sure to use the correct forms.

1. Mark looked _____ with his hair uncombed, his face unshaven, and his shirt untucked.

2. In many cultures, being strong and brave are characteristics often connected to _____.

3. For her final art project, Julie _____ a statue of a horse.

4. In some countries it has become _____ for women to have careers; however, in others it has not.

5. Major companies will _____ from the government cutting big business taxes.

6. Christmas is a time of year when _____ is strong.

What's Your Opinion?

A. People do many different things to look good. Are these acceptable for men, women, or both? Check (✔) your answers.

	Men	Women	Both
1. Spend a lot of money on clothing.	☐	☐	☐
2. Take mud baths.	☐	☐	☐
3. Paint fingernails.	☐	☐	☐
4. Take an hour to get ready in the morning.	☐	☐	☐
5. Wear cosmetics.	☐	☐	☐

B. Discuss your answers with a partner. Give reasons for your answers.

Part 2 Changing Faces

Before Reading

Discuss this question.

If you could change one thing about your looks, what would it be? Why?

...... eyes   ...... nose   ...... ears   ...... other: _____

Fluency Strategy: Previewing and Predicting

> Previewing means looking at the text title and images (photos, graphs, etc.)
> *before* you start reading. After previewing, you should try to predict what the
> text will be about. Previewing and predicting before you start reading can
> help you improve your understanding of the text when you read.

**A. Look at the title and photo to predict the text topic. What do you think this article
will be about? Circle the best answer.**

1. A new makeup fashion trend.
2. A trend in plastic surgery.
3. A trend in health.

B. Read the whole text quickly. Record your reading time below and on the chart on page 193.

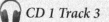
CD 1 Track 3

Start: _____
Finish: _____
Reading Time: _____

Changing Faces

1   Aiko Maekawa, age 24, once thought of
herself as just a shy, plain office worker.
Then one day she made a discovery which
changed everything. When she used glue
to hold up her eyelids, men took notice of
her. The rounder, wider appearance of her
eyes seemed to make her more attractive to
others. "Men started to ask me out on dates,"
she says. "So my confidence grew, and I
became more outgoing."

2   Aiko enjoyed the new attention but
worried that people would discover her
secret. She had to constantly reapply glue
and avoid being outside on hot days, fearing
that her secret would melt away.

3   But now, after a minor surgery that took
less than 15 minutes, Aiko can go on with
her active social life stress-free. With rounder
eyes and a more defined nose bridge, she has
the face she's always wanted.

4   To look good these days, sometimes
wearing the hottest designer clothes or
getting the latest, hip hairstyle is not enough.
More people are seeking better looks,

confidence, and even success, through plastic surgery. Changes like Aiko's are happening all over Asia.

5   In Japan, small, quick surgeries are popular, with many clinics making 100 million dollars a year on these procedures. In Taiwan, the number of surgeries has grown rapidly over the past several years with about a million performed last year alone. Thailand advertises plastic surgery tours for foreign visitors in order to profit from the growing trend.

6   In South Korea, not only are adults changing their faces, but kids are too. Teenagers have become experts in plastic surgery, being able to use technical words and request specific surgical methods. Their parents are often supportive, realizing that good looks can help their children to be competitive and successful in society. What is a popular gift for high school graduates? Larger eyes.

7   In China, as the country has grown more prosperous, so has the focus on beauty and acceptance of plastic surgery in the mainstream culture. Just a few years ago, at a beauty pageant held only for people who had plastic surgery, China's first Miss Artificial Beauty was crowned.

8   Today, attaining beauty does cost money, and people are spending a lot of it on surgeries. In fact, enhanced beauty through plastic surgery has become a sign of wealth. When the economy gets stronger, people improve their looks as a way to show off their money.

9   Others hope that plastic surgery will help them gain more success and wealth. Xin Li, an accountant in Beijing, China, says that with so many people in his country, surgically improving one's appearance has become a way to stand out. "If there are five people with the same abilities going for the same job, it's likely that the better-looking person will succeed," he says.

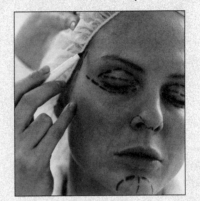

10   Although surgery may be an indication of wealth, many people are still looking for beauty at a bargain. Apkujong in Seoul, Korea, has over 400 clinics and is a popular destination for foreign visitors wanting surgeries at inexpensive prices. Many travelers come on plastic surgery tours offering cheap packages which include the surgery as well as hotel, travel costs, and sightseeing. The price of such a package can be the same as the cost of the surgery alone in other countries.

11   Shizuka Nishimoto, age 45 from Japan, is on a three-day visit for some shopping, sightseeing, a face-lift[1], and liposuction[2]. "This vacation is for me," she says. "I'm unhappy with my weight, and want to see a younger me when I look in the mirror. While I'm here, I'm glad I can also enjoy being a tourist. I'll return home to my family with some souvenirs, and a new me."

1 face-lift surgery to remove wrinkles in the face
2 liposuction surgery to remove fat

Checking Fluency and Comprehension

A. Mark these statements true (T) or false (F). Do not look back at the text.

.... **1.** This article is mainly about the cost of plastic surgery.

.... **2.** Parents in Korea are against their children having surgery.

.... **3.** Plastic surgery is popular in China, but not in Thailand.

.... **4.** Plastic surgery is a way to show you have money.

.... **5.** Some people get plastic surgery to become more successful.

B. Check your answers with a partner. Record your score on page 193.

Expanding Vocabulary

A. Synonyms are words with a similar meaning. Look in the passage to find synonyms of the words below.

1. continuously .... (par. 2)

2. operation .... (par. 3)

3. looking for .... (par. 4)

4. successful .... (par. 7)

5. achieving .... (par. 8)

6. improved .... (par. 8)

B. Fill in the blanks with the synonyms you wrote in A. Be sure to use the correct forms.

1. He is a good businessman who runs a .... company.

2. Eyelid .... is a very common procedure in many countries.

3. I'm currently .... employment as a waiter.

4. It rained .... for five straight days before the sun finally came out.

5. The best way to .... our goal is to work together.

6. This laptop has a/an .... screen, which is why it costs more.

What's Your Opinion?

Discuss the questions.

1. Is plastic surgery popular in your country? If so, what kinds of procedures are popular?

2. In what situations do you think plastic surgery is acceptable?

3. In what situations do you think plastic surgery is unacceptable?

4. What is one physical trait you would never change about yourself?

5. How do you feel about aging? Will it be important for you to look young, even as you get older?

Increasing Fluency

Read the paragraph quickly; don't stop to think about the missing words. Mark the statements below true (T) or false (F).

Looking Young

As we get older, we'll do anything to still look XXXXX. Youth and beauty are XXXXX in our society. As a result, there are many ways people can try to XXXXX their young looks. For example, we have many XXXXX, such as anti-aging creams and lotions that will prevent skin XXXXX by the sun. Also, we have XXXXX to hide wrinkles, add color, and give our skin a healthy, young appearance. Finally, for some people, cosmetic XXXXX is the solution!

.... 1. Looking young is important to some people.

.... 2. Skin damage from the sun may make us look older.

.... 3. We don't have many products to help us hide our age.

.... 4. Plastic surgery is the most common way to look younger.

Extensive Reading 1

The Picture of Dorian Gray

Introduction

This extract from an Oxford *Bookworms* reader gives you the opportunity to read more in English. The more you read, the faster and more fluent you will become. *The Picture of Dorian Gray* is set in England in the late 19th century. It is the story of a young man, Dorian Gray, whose picture was painted by an artist, Basil Hallward. The extract you will read starts as Lord Henry Wotton and Basil Hallward are discussing the painting, which has just been completed.

Before Reading

A. What do you think will happen in the extract? Check (✔) your answers.

    1. Basil and his good friend, Lord Henry Wotton, talk about Basil's painting.

    2. Lord Henry thinks the painting of Dorian Gray is terrible.

    3. Lord Henry meets Dorian Gray, who is a very handsome young man.

    4. Lord Henry tells Dorian Gray that his beauty will not last.

B. Now read the extract to see what happens.

🎧 *CD 1 Track 4*

Words

Through the open windows of the room came the rich scent of summer flowers. Lord Henry Wotton lay back in his chair and smoked his cigarette. Beyond the soft sounds of the garden he could just hear the noise of London.

In the center of the room there was a portrait of a very beautiful young man, and in front of it stood the artist himself, Basil Hallward.

50

"It's your best work, Basil, the best portrait that you've ever painted," said Lord Henry lazily. "You must send it to the best art gallery in London."

"No," Basil said slowly. "No, I won't send it anywhere."

100

Lord Henry was surprised. "But my dear Basil, why not?" he asked. "What strange people you artists are! You want to be famous, but then you're not happy when you *are* famous. It's bad when people talk about you—but it's much worse when they *don't* talk about you."

"I know you'll laugh at me," replied Basil, "but I can't exhibit the picture in an art gallery. I've put too much of myself into it."

Lord Henry laughed. "Too much of yourself into it! You don't look like him at all. He has a fair and beautiful

face. And you—well, you look intelligent, of course, but with your strong face and black hair, you are not beautiful."

"You don't understand me, Harry," replied Basil. (Lord Henry's friends always called him Harry.) "Of course I'm not like him," Basil continued. "In fact, I prefer not to be beautiful. Dorian Gray's beautiful face will perhaps bring him danger and trouble."

"Dorian Gray? Is that his name?" asked Lord Henry.

"Yes. But I didn't want to tell you."

"Why not?"

"Oh, I can't explain," said Basil. "When I like people a lot, I never tell their names to my other friends. I love secrets, that's all."

"Of course," agreed his friend. "Life is much more exciting when you have secrets. For example, I never know where my wife is, and my wife never knows what I'm doing. When we meet—and we do meet sometimes—we tell each other crazy stories, and we pretend that they're true."

"You pretend all the time, Harry," said Basil. "I think that you're probably a very good husband, but you like to hide your true feelings."

"Oh, don't be so serious, Basil," smiled Lord Henry. "Let's go into the garden."

* * *

Basil goes into the garden with Lord Henry. They talk about the painting and about Dorian Gray. Then Dorian arrives at the house, and Basil introduces him to Lord Henry. Lord Henry tells Dorian that he should value his youth and good looks, as youth is the most important thing in the world. He warns Dorian that time and age are his enemies.

* * *

250

300

350

400

450

In the house Basil Hallward stood in front of the portrait of Dorian Gray. "It's finished," he said. He wrote his name in the corner of the picture.

Lord Henry studied the picture carefully. "Yes," he said. "It's your best work. It's excellent. Mr. Gray, come and look at yourself."

Dorian looked at the picture for a long time. He smiled as he saw the beautiful face in front of him, and for a moment he felt happy. But then he remembered Lord Henry's words. "How long," he thought, "will I look like

the picture? Time will steal my beauty from me. I will grow old, but the picture will always be young." And his heart grew cold with fear.

"Don't you like it, Dorian?" asked Basil at last.

"Of course he likes it," said Lord Henry. "It's a very fine work of art. I'd like to buy it myself." 600

"It's not mine to sell, Harry. The picture is Dorian's."

"I wish," cried Dorian suddenly, "I wish that I could always stay young and that the picture could grow old."

Lord Henry laughed. "I don't think you would like that, 650 Basil, would you?"

"No, I wouldn't like it at all," agreed Basil with a smile.

Dorian turned, his face red and angry. "Yes, you like your art better than your friends," he said to Basil. "How long will you like me? Only while I'm beautiful, I suppose. Lord Henry is right. Youth is the most important 700 thing in the world. Oh, why did you paint this picture? Why should it stay young while I grow old? I wish the picture could change, and I could stay as I am. I would give anything, yes, anything, for that." He hid his face in 750 his hands.

"Dorian, Dorian!" said Basil unhappily. "Don't talk like that. You're my dearest friend." He turned to Lord Henry. "What have you been teaching him?" he asked angrily. "Why didn't you go away when I asked you?"

Lord Henry smiled. "It's the real Dorian Gray— 800 that's all."

Basil turned and walked quickly over to the portrait. "It's my best work, but now I hate it. I will destroy it now, before it destroys our friendship." He picked up a long knife.

But Dorian was there before him. "No, Basil, don't! You can't destroy it. That would be murder!" 850

"So," said Basil coldly, "you've decided that you like the portrait after all."

"Like it?" said Dorian. "I'm in love with it. I cannot live without it."

Extract from *The Picture of Dorian Gray,* Bookworms Library, Oxford University Press.

After Reading

Answer the questions.

1. Why didn't Basil want to exhibit his painting of Dorian Gray?

....

2. Why didn't Basil want to tell Lord Henry about his friend Dorian?

....

3. What did Dorian wish for when he saw the painting of himself?

....

4. Why did Basil want to destroy his picture of Dorian?

....

Thinking About the Story

Answer the questions.

1. Did you enjoy reading the extract? Do you want to read more about Dorian, Lord Henry, and Basil?
2. Do you think Lord Henry is an evil man?
3. What do you think will happen to Dorian Gray?

Timed Repeated Reading

How many words can you read in one minute? Follow the instructions to practice increasing your reading speed.

1. Time yourself. Read the extract for one minute. When you stop, underline the last word you read and write "first" in the margin.
2. Go back to the beginning of the extract. Read again for one minute. Try to read faster this time. When you stop, underline the last word you read and write "second" in the margin.
3. Go back to the beginning of the extract. Read again for one minute. Try to read even faster this time. When you stop, underline the last word you read and write "third" in the margin.
4. Count the number of words you read each time. Record the three numbers on the Timed Repeated Reading Chart on page 193.

Unit 2

Travel

Discuss the questions.

1. What was the last trip you took? Where did you go? What did you do? Who did you go with?

2. If you could travel anywhere in the world, where would you go? Why?

This unit is about traveling. In Part 1, you will read a newspaper article about one woman's travel mistake. In Part 2, you will read an advice column about preventing problems with travel companions. The unit is followed by Extensive Reading 2, which is an extract from a book called *The Wind in the Willows*. It is the classic story of the travels of three animals: the Mole, the Rat, and the Toad.

Before Reading

Discuss the questions.

1. What is the worst trip you've ever taken?
2. What is the worst mistake you've ever made when traveling?

Comprehension Strategy: Summarizing

> Summarizing is writing the main points communicated by a text in much fewer words. When we summarize, we write only the essential information and leave out any points of lesser importance.

A. Read the text. Complete the summary with information from the text.

Kumiko Tsuchida, a 40-year-old .... was trying to get

from England to .... When she asked people how to get to

...., they instead directed her to .... ,

a small English town. By 2:00 A.M. she was .... She was given

.... for the night and sent to the ....

for help in the morning.

B. Read the text again and answer the questions that follow.

🎧 *CD 1 Track 5*

Travel Mistakes and Miscommunications

1   *Travelers have all made mistakes at one time or another. For example, we can sympathize with the traveler who doesn't know the exact rate of currency exchange while on a trip to a foreign country. As a result, she may pay double the price she expects for a hotel stay but not realize it until she gets her credit card bill the next month. Or, maybe a traveler forgets his passport and is kindly reminded by the immigration officer[1] at the airport immediately before the flight departure. Running home to get his passport and still making the flight on time is not an option!*

2   *When it comes to communicating in a foreign language, there is clear room for misunderstanding. One such major miscommunication happened to Kumiko Tsuchida, a Japanese tourist visiting a friend*

in England. Read about her travel mistake in the newspaper article below:

3 Tourist Bound for Turkey Ends Up in Torquay

A Japanese tourist who wanted to catch a flight to the country of Turkey was put on a train to the town of Torquay in southwest England after asking for directions.

4   Kumiko Tsuchida, who was on her first visit to Britain, arrived in Torquay at midnight. She was convinced that she had been through the English Channel Tunnel and was now in Istanbul, Turkey.

5   Mrs. Tsuchida, 40, who taught Japanese at Istanbul University, knew very little English. First, things started to go wrong when she left the house of a friend in London to catch a train to Heathrow airport. At the train station, she inquired about the best way to travel to the country of Turkey.

6   Speaking through an interpreter, Mrs. Tsuchida said: "I told the staff that I wanted to go to Turkey. I kept saying 'Turkey, Turkey.' But because of my pronunciation, they put me on a train to Torquay. I thought it was a long way to the airport but when I asked people 'Turkey? Turkey?' they told me I was on the right train."

7   "She told officers that she had been on the train so long, she genuinely believed she was in Turkey already," said a spokesman for the police.

8   She was found wandering in the streets at 2 A.M. by the police. They started an investigation involving social services, a home for the elderly, a travel agent, and the Japanese embassy.

9   Social services received a call from police shortly after 2 A.M. "They had a lost and

Torquay, England

exhausted lady from Japan who needed a bed for the night," said a spokesman. "We were happy to oblige. She was too tired to eat and went straight to bed."

10   Mrs. Tsuchida slept well through the night, and then was handed over to the Japanese Embassy in the morning. After the long, mistaken journey, she found herself £26 short of the one-way airfare to Istanbul. However, the Heathrow press corps raised the extra money for her ticket, so she was able to make the flight successfully.

11   "What happened to me was caused by my mistakes," she said. "I did not have any maps or books and did not know where to go."

12   *Of course, Mrs. Tsuchida's story of miscommunication is a bit extreme. Not many travelers would mistakenly end up in the wrong country! However, her story is an example that shows mishaps and miscommunications are possible, especially when traveling in a foreign country. In her future travels, Mrs. Tsuchida will surely not forget her maps and guidebooks.*

1 immigration officer a person who checks passports and controls entry to a country

Checking Comprehension

A. Answer the questions.

1. How old was Mrs. Tsuchida? ....

2. What was Mrs. Tsuchida's job? ....

3. Where did Mrs. Tsuchida want to go? ....

4. Why did station staff put Mrs. Tsuchida on a train to Torquay?

   ....

5. How much more money did Mrs. Tsuchida need to buy a plane ticket?

   ....

6. Who offered Mrs. Tsuchida a bed for the night after she got lost?

   ....

B. These sentences are false. Correct the facts.

1. When traveling, it's very rare to make travel mistakes.

   ....

2. Mrs. Tsuchida wanted to go to Torquay, but mistakenly ended up in Turkey.

   ....

3. At the airport, Mrs. Tsuchida asked for directions to Turkey.

   ....

4. Mrs. Tsuchida had a poor English vocabulary, so the staff misunderstood her.

   ....

5. Mrs. Tsuchida was found lost in the streets at 12 A.M. by police.

   ....

6. The police raised extra money for her train ticket to Turkey.

   ....

Looking at Vocabulary in Context

A. Find the words in bold in the text. Circle the correct definitions.

1. **Sympathize with** (par. 1) means to *remember / understand* how someone feels.
2. **Convinced** (par. 4) means *sure / not sure* about something.
3. **Inquired** (par. 5) means *asked / argued* about something.
4. **Genuinely** (par. 7) means *sadly / honestly*.
5. **Exhausted** (par. 9) means *very tired / very angry*.
6. **Mishaps** (par. 12) are *accidents / arguments*.

B. Fill in the blanks with the words in bold from A. Be sure to use the correct forms.

1. I'm _____ after staying up last night studying for exams.
2. I used to work three different jobs, so I can _____ your difficult schedule.
3. The young boy felt bad, and _____ apologized for his mistake.
4. After many dangerous _____, the chemical company was finally shut down.
5. Sue called her travel agent and _____ about a flight on the 25th, but nothing was available.
6. He lies a lot, so I'm not _____ he is telling the truth now.

What's Your Opinion?

A. Use these questions and one of your own to interview people in your class. Find someone who answers "Yes" to each question and write the person's name.

Classmate

1. Have you ever traveled to a foreign country? _____
2. Have you ever made a mistake when traveling? _____
3. Have you ever used a second language when traveling? _____
4. Have you ever gotten lost when traveling? _____
5. _____? _____

B. Tell the rest of the class what you found out.

Part 2 | Dealing with your Travel Companion

Before Reading

Discuss the questions

1. Do you prefer to travel alone or with others? Why?
2. Who did you travel with last? Where did you go? What did you do?

Fluency Strategy: Skimming for the Main Idea

> Skimming is reading key parts of a text quickly to understand the main idea. First, read the title and subtitles. Then read the first and last paragraphs quickly. If you still do not understand the main idea, then quickly read the first and last sentences in the other paragraphs. Read quickly. Ignore unknown words and details.

A. Use the strategy to skim the text. Circle the main idea.

1. It's better to learn about your travel partner before the trip than after.
2. There are a number of things to watch out for when choosing a travel partner.
3. We should take steps to avoid problems with travel partners.

B. Read the whole text quickly. Record your reading time below and on the chart on page 193.

CD 1 Track 6

Start: _____
Finish: _____
Reading Time: _____

Dealing with your Travel Companion[1]

1   No matter how carefully you plan a trip with a friend, a romantic interest, or family member, there will probably be conflicts along the way. Even after the dates, destination, and length of the trip are decided, and the tickets have been bought, there's still the chance that problems could happen on the trip.

2   Here are a few tips to help you solve problems that may come up between you and your travel companion:

3   **Plan the trip together:** Sometimes one person takes the lead and plans the trip to fit his or her interests. Planning together allows for a more diverse and balanced vacation. "Some people like to sightsee a lot, other people don't. Some people want to walk, some people would rather use public transportation," said Dorlene Kaplan, president of ShawGuides, a publisher of guides to educational travel and career programs.

4   "So it's important to find out how compatible you are in terms of the things that you're going to be doing, the places that you're going to be going, how much time you're going to be spending together," said Kaplan.

5   **Be clear about budgets:** Vacation time is not exempt from arguments over money. Different budgets and feelings about spending can leave travel companions at odds[2] over what to do next, said Andrew Sharp, a psychiatric nurse practitioner at a clinic in New Orleans, Louisiana. "Some people will want to go to an expensive restaurant when others weren't prepared to do that," he said. Discussing budgets before the trip will reduce misunderstandings and help travelers see when there's extra money to spend. Kaplan recommends deciding how shared costs will be handled—will they be split equally as you go or calculated at the end of the trip?

6   **Find out about lifestyle:** Differences in lifestyle can be challenging if they haven't been discussed in advance. "There's nothing worse than being in the room and awake at 6 A.M. when your companion wanted to sleep until noon," Sharp said. "Sleep patterns can be very disruptive to people that don't have the same pattern," he said.

7   The same can be said for dietary and other restrictions. Knowing those differences in advance helps people adapt to each other more quickly. Drinking habits may also be an issue, as alcohol tends to increase conflicts.

8   **Be aware of coping strategies:**[3] Ask questions and use your understanding of your companion's coping strategies—how they may respond to stressful situations. Is this person usually patient and flexible?

9   Sharp recommends asking your travel companion about their best and worst trips. What happened? How did that person respond? Knowing a little about how your companion deals with difficult situations can be helpful. "It's not as bad if you've kind of predicted that that's how they're going to behave in certain situations, as if it hits you by surprise," Sharp said.

10   **Compromise:** Try to compromise in order to have a good time. "Agree to disagree. Do you really want to use your energy feeling anger on your vacation when you should be relaxing and enjoying it?" Sharp said. He recommends buying travel journals for yourself and your travel companions. Writing in journals can be a way to reflect on the trip and relieve some of the frustration that may come up.

11   **Take a break:** Split up when tensions are high and your interests are different. Be sure to set a time and meeting place and have a backup meeting set in case of an unforeseen delay. "People tend to feel like they have to stick together when they are together on a trip," Sharp said. "And anybody with someone breathing their air, so to speak, 24 hours a day needs a break from the other person."

1 travel companion a person who travels with another
2 to be at odds to disagree
3 coping strategies ways people deal with problems or stresses

Checking Fluency and Comprehension

A. Complete the sentences. Do not look at the text.

1. According to the passage, when you plan a trip, you should ....
   a. use a travel agent.
   b. plan together with your travel companion.

2. Before a trip, it's important to discuss travel budgets because ....
   a. spending different amounts of money can cause disagreements.
   b. it's difficult to save money when traveling.

3. Lifestyle differences can cause travel problems because ....
   a. different people could have different sleeping patterns.
   b. most people enjoy sleeping a lot when on vacation.

4. To understand your companion's coping strategies, you could ....
   a. ask questions about his or her best and worst vacation.
   b. each keep a travel journal.

5. According to the passage, if your travel interests are different you should
   ....
   a. try to take a break and meet later.
   b. try to agree on a restaurant and eat together.

B. Check your answers with a partner. Record your score on page 193.

Expanding Vocabulary

A. Find the adjectives or nouns in the text that are related to these words.

1. compatibility .... (par. 4)
2. psychiatry .... (par. 5)
3. disrupt .... (par. 6)
4. restrict .... (par. 7)
5. flex .... (par. 8)
6. tense .... (par. 11)

B. **Match the words with the definitions. Fill in the blanks with the correct form of the words you found in A.**

1. .... —a feeling of anger between people

2. .... —causing trouble; stopping something from happening as usual

3. .... —able to exist or work together successfully

4. .... —a limitation; not being able to have or do something

5. .... —having to do with the science of the mind

6. .... —able to easily change according to the situation

What's Your Opinion?

Discuss the questions.

1. What are the advantages of traveling with a companion instead of alone?
2. What kind of person do you enjoy traveling with?
3. What kind of person do you least enjoy traveling with?
4. What kinds of problems could come up between you and a travel companion?
5. How would you cope with a difficult travel companion?

Increasing Fluency

Scan the line to find the phrase on the left. Phrases may appear more than once. Can you finish in 15 seconds?

	a	b	c	d	e
1. back out	back in	back up	back out	back off	back out
2. deal with	dealer	deal out	peal out	deal with	deal down
3. come up	come out	come up	come over	come in	come up
4. at odds	at odds	odds are	odds out	at odds	poor odds
5. find out	find out	feel out	find it	freak out	find out
6. in fear	in front	in fear	in fact	in fear	in fact
7. adapt to	adapt to	adopt to	adept at	adapt for	adapt to
8. kind of	kind to	kind of	kinder to	kinds of	kids of

Extensive Reading 2

The Wind in the Willows

Introduction

This extract from an Oxford *Bookworms* reader gives you the opportunity to read more in English. The more you read, the faster and more fluent you will become. *The Wind in the Willows* is a classic story of the adventures of the Mole, the Rat, and the Toad. The extract you will read starts as the Mole and the Rat decide to take a boat ride to visit the Toad. They find that the Toad has a new hobby.

Before Reading

A. What do you think you will find out in the extract? Check (✔) your answers.

.... **1.** The Toad's new hobby is growing roses.

.... **2.** The Toad is bored with boating and wants to do something different.

.... **3.** The Rat doesn't want to join the Toad in traveling around the countryside.

.... **4.** All three start out on the open road.

B. Now read the extract to see what happens.

🎧 *CD 1 Track 7*

Words

One bright summer morning the Mole and the Rat were out on the river bank, watching the world go by. The Rat was writing a song and was singing quietly to himself as he tried different words.

"Ratty," said the Mole, "could I ask you something?"

"Mmm," the Rat said, not really listening. "Sky, fly, high, die, why . . . Oh dear! What did you say, Mole?"

50

"Will you take me to visit Mr. Toad? I've heard so much about him, and I do want to meet him."

"Why, of course," said the Rat kindly. "Get the boat out, and we'll row up there now. Toad's always happy to see his friends."

100

"He must be a very nice animal," said the Mole, as he got into the boat and took the oars.

"He's the best of animals," replied the Rat. "Kind, friendly—not very smart, perhaps, and sometimes he's just a little bit boastful, but he's a good fellow really."

The Mole rowed hard up the river and in a while they came to a large red house with beautiful gardens reaching down to the water's edge.

"There's Toad Hall," said the Rat. "It's a lovely old house—Toad is very rich, you know, and this is really one of the nicest houses on the river. But we never say that to Toad, of course."

150

200

They left their boat by the boathouse at the end of the garden. The boathouse was full of expensive boats, which looked new and mostly unused.

The Rat looked around him. "I see that all the boats are out of the water," he said. "I suppose Toad has finished with boating now and has some new interest to amuse him."

They walked over the grass toward the house and soon found the Toad, resting in a garden-chair and carefully studying a large map.

"Wonderful!" he cried, as he saw them. "You're just the fellow that I wanted to see, Ratty." He jumped up and came toward them, talking all the time, and gave the Rat no time to introduce the Mole. "I need you very much—both of you. You've got to help me. It's most important!"

"It's about your rowing, I suppose," said the Rat, keeping his face very serious. "You *will* learn to do it in the end, you know, if you're patient and work hard and—"

"Oh, bother boats!" the Toad said angrily. "I've finished with boats. Silly way to pass the time. No, I've discovered the real thing—the best way, the *only* way, to spend one's life. Come with me, dear Ratty, and your kind friend too, and I will show you!"

He took them around to the other side of the house, and there they saw a shiny new gipsy caravan. It had yellow and green sides, and red wheels.

"There you are!" cried the Toad. "There's real life for you. The open road, the fields, the hills . . . villages, towns, cities! Here today, off to a different place tomorrow! Travel, change, interest—the world in front of you!"

The Mole was very interested and excited, and followed the Toad inside the caravan to look around. But the Rat shook his head and waited outside.

When they came down the steps again, the Toad was still talking excitedly to the Mole. "So you see, everything is ready for when we start this afternoon."

"What was that?" said the Rat slowly. "Did you say 'we' and 'start' and 'this afternoon'?"

"Now, dear good old Ratty," said Toad quickly, "don't talk in that angry voice. You know you've *got* to come. You can't stay by your boring old river all your life. I want to show you the world!"

"I don't care," said the Rat calmly. "I'm not coming, and that's final. I'm going to stay by my old river, and what's more, Mole's going to stay with me, aren't you, Mole?"

"Of course I am," said the Mole bravely. But his face looked sad. Poor Mole! He thought that life in a caravan on the open road would be an exciting adventure.

The Rat saw his sad face and felt worried. He liked his friends to be happy and he could see that the Mole really wanted to go.

Toad watched them both carefully. "Come in and have some lunch," he said pleasantly, "and we'll talk it over."

During lunch—which was excellent, of course, because everything at Toad Hall always was—the Toad talked and talked. He was full of wonderful plans. How interesting each day would be! What adventures the three friends would have together! Ah, the happiness of the traveling life!

In the end, of course, the Rat agreed to go, and by the evening they found themselves on a lonely hillside, miles from home. It had been a golden afternoon, and even the Rat had enjoyed the journey so far. Only the old gray horse was not very happy. He had to do all the hard work of pulling the caravan, and he was not at all pleased about it.

550

600

650

700

750

800

The next morning the Toad was still sleeping deeply when the other two got up. They shook him very hard but couldn't wake him, so they had to do all the work. The Rat took care of the horse, lit the fire, and did last night's dishes. The Mole walked to the nearest village, a long way away, to get milk and eggs and bread, which the Toad had, of course, forgotten to bring. And when at last the Toad got up, he said what a pleasant easy life it was on the open road.

Extract from *The Wind in the Willows,* Bookworms Library, Oxford University Press.

After Reading

Answer the questions.

1. What was the Toad's previous hobby?

....

2. How does the Toad plan to travel and see the world?

....

3. Who didn't want to go on the trip at first?

....

4. Who was the last to get up in the morning?

....

Thinking About the Story

Answer the questions.

1. Did you enjoy reading the extract? Do you want to read more about the Rat, the Mole, and the Toad?
2. What do you think will happen to them on the open road?
3. What other adventures might the Rat, the Mole, and the Toad have?

Timed Repeated Reading

How many words can you read in one minute? Follow the instructions to practice increasing your reading speed.

1. Time yourself. Read the extract for one minute. When you stop, underline the last word you read and write "first" in the margin.
2. Go back to the beginning of the extract. Read again for one minute. Try to read faster this time. When you stop, underline the last word you read and write "second" in the margin.
3. Go back to the beginning of the extract. Read again for one minute. Try to read even faster this time. When you stop, underline the last word you read and write "third" in the margin.
4. Count the number of words you read each time. Record the three numbers on the Timed Repeated Reading Chart on page 193.

Unit 3

Lying

Discuss the questions.

1. Pinocchio is a famous folktale about a puppet whose nose grows every time he tells a lie. Do you know any folktales or sayings about lying?

2. Are you good at knowing when another person is telling a lie to you, or not? Give an example.

This unit is about lying—not telling the truth. In Part 1, you will read an essay about lying. In Part 2, you will read about how to tell when someone is lying. The unit is followed by Extensive Reading 3, which is an extract from a book called *The Railway Children*. It is about the lives of three children whose father is imprisoned. They are only told that he will be "away for some time" and that they are all going to "play at being poor for a while."

Before Reading

Discuss the questions.

  1. Do you think all human beings lie?

  2. What would it be like if you could only tell the truth all the time?

Comprehension Strategy: Recognizing the Author's Purpose

Part of understanding a text is recognizing the author's purpose or reason for writing it. These purposes include to:
• inform • persuade • entertain • instruct • advise • argue

A. Read the text. Use the strategy to find the author's purpose. Check (✔) your answer.

...... **1.** to inform the reader about lying

...... **2.** to entertain the reader using the ways people lie

...... **3.** to argue about lying

...... **4.** to instruct the reader about how to avoid lying

B. Read the whole text and answer the questions that follow.

🎧 *CD 1 Track 8*

On the Decay of the Art of Lying

1   *Samuel Langhorne Clemens, also known as Mark Twain, was an American writer, journalist, and humorist who won a worldwide audience for his stories of the youthful adventures of Tom Sawyer and Huckleberry Finn. The following essay is based on parts of a humorous speech he once gave on the subject of lying.*

2   Don't get me wrong, ladies and gentlemen. I do not mean to suggest that the custom of lying has declined. Lying is something that humans have always done and will always do. It would be an impossible task to stop people from enjoying their favorite hobby of lying. My complaint simply concerns the decay of the art of lying. It's obvious to every educated person that people lie more poorly today than they ever have! You just can't find people who lie as well as they did in the good old days. It's a terrible situation that truly saddens me.

3   Most sensible people agree that lying is something we cannot do without. To try to live without lying would be foolishness. Since lying is necessary, it makes sense that we should lie well. As we know, anyone who

wishes to do something well needs to study it. Therefore it is obvious that the subject of lying should be taught in the public schools and perhaps in the newspapers.

4   Now let's consider what the philosophers say about lying. Consider the wise old saying: "Children and fools always speak the truth." The meaning of this old saying should be obvious to anyone. It means that adults and wise people never speak the truth! Another well-known saying goes: "The truth should not be spoken at all times." How very true! I mean, can you imagine living with someone who spoke nothing but the truth from sunrise to sunset? How unbearable it would be.

5   Fortunately, nobody has to live with such a person, a chronic truth-teller, a person who never tells a lie. This is because no such person exists, and no such person ever has existed. There are, of course, people who think that they never lie, but it is not so. Everybody lies, and if people keep quiet, their eyes, gestures, and attitude continue to convey deception—and on purpose! And let's not forget that just in keeping silent it is of course possible to hide the truth. This type of lying I call silent lying. Are you familiar with it?

6   So now that we all agree that lying is universal and that all human beings do it, I think the wisest thing we can do is to carefully and thoroughly train ourselves in the fine art of lying before it decays any further. And let's use our lying for the purposes of good, not evil! Let's lie for the

Mark Twain

advantage of others and not our own. We can lie gracefully and graciously, not awkwardly and clumsily. There's no need to be nervous about it any longer. Let all the skillful liars come out into the open and create a better world through their lying. May the golden age of lying begin!

7   Then again, maybe I've gone too far. Joking aside, I do think we need to examine the role that lying plays in our personal lives and in the life of society. By studying how we lie, I think we might learn a great deal about ourselves and maybe even improve the society we live in.

Checking Comprehension

Answer the questions.

1. How does the author achieve humor in his essay?
   a. By being light and silly about a serious topic.
   b. By taking an unexpected position on the topic.
   c. By saying things that aren't true.

2. What does the author write about today's liars?
   a. They do not lie as well as they used to.
   b. They lie much better than they used to.
   c. They lie about as well as they used to.

3. According to the author, what is the meaning of the saying, "Children and fools always speak the truth"?
   a. We should all try to be like children and fools.
   b. Children are very similar to fools.
   c. Adults and wise people never speak the truth.

4. What does the author tell us about people who never tell lies?
   a. They are very boring.
   b. They do not exist.
   c. They dislike liars.

5. How does the author suggest that people should lie?
   a. Humanely and charitably.
   b. Silently and sneakily.
   c. Awkwardly and clumsily.

6. Which statement probably expresses the author's true feelings?
   a. Lying is admirable and always appropriate.
   b. We should always tell the truth.
   c. Everyone lies, but sometimes lying should be avoided.

Looking at Vocabulary in Context

A. Find the words in bold in the text. Circle the correct definition.

1. If the amount of something has **declined** (par. 2), it has gone *up* / *down*.

2. When **decay** (par. 2) happens to something, it gets *worse* / *better*.

3. A person who is **sensible** (par. 3) is *realistic* / *foolish*.

4. A **chronic** (par. 5) problem *stays for a long time* / *soon passes*.

5. To **convey** (par. 5) a message is to *communicate* / *eliminate* it.

6. **Deception** (par. 5) is another word for *the truth* / *a lie*.

B. Complete the sentences with the words in bold from A. Be sure to use the correct forms.

1. Sandra had to go to the doctor over 20 times to cure her _____ illness.

2. Parents need to _____ to their children that lying is wrong.

3. In spite of her _____, the police finally found out that she stole the money.

4. The number of people who attend movies has continued to _____ in recent years.

5. Marco is a _____ person who works hard and saves money for the future.

6. If the _____ of the political situation continues, the two countries may go to war.

What's Your Opinion?

A. Answer the questions.

1. Who is the best liar you know?

2. Do you think that we must always tell the truth?

3. Should students be taught to lie carefully and cleverly?

4. Have you ever been caught in a lie?

5. In what situations is it important to lie?

B. Discuss your answers in small groups.

Before Reading

Are the statements true or false?

1. How do people sometimes show that they are lying?
2. How can you be sure that someone is telling the truth?

Fluency Strategy: Scanning

Scanning is searching a text very quickly to find information you want. Don't read every word. Move your eyes across the text until you find what you're looking for. Scanning saves time by allowing you to jump directly to the information you want.

A. Scan the text for the noun phrases. Match them with the information.

...... **1.** the age of four or five   **a.** lying once or twice a day

...... **2.** change in voice   **b.** we start telling lies

...... **3.** a nation of liars   **c.** being overly defensive

...... **4.** something to hide   **d.** a common sign of lying

B. Read the whole article quickly. Record your reading time below and on the chart on page 193.

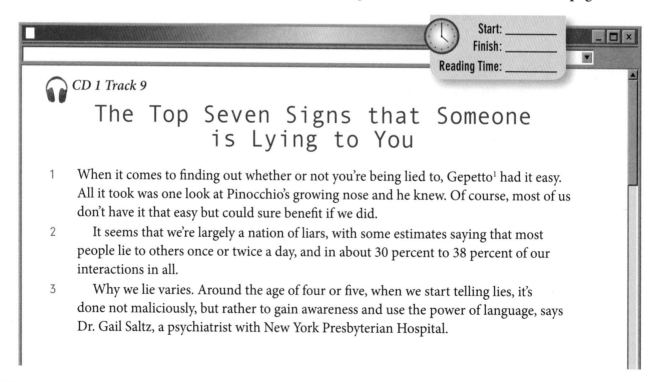

Start: _____
Finish: _____
Reading Time: _____

CD 1 Track 9

The Top Seven Signs that Someone is Lying to You

1   When it comes to finding out whether or not you're being lied to, Gepetto[1] had it easy. All it took was one look at Pinocchio's growing nose and he knew. Of course, most of us don't have it that easy but could sure benefit if we did.

2   It seems that we're largely a nation of liars, with some estimates saying that most people lie to others once or twice a day, and in about 30 percent to 38 percent of our interactions in all.

3   Why we lie varies. Around the age of four or five, when we start telling lies, it's done not maliciously, but rather to gain awareness and use the power of language, says Dr. Gail Saltz, a psychiatrist with New York Presbyterian Hospital.

4　　Later on, we lie to get things we want, for personal gain, or to stay out of trouble. We tell "white lies" to protect other's feelings, and then there are the pathological liars among us, the people who feel compelled to lie no matter what.

5　　So, with liars all around us (don't lie—we ALL lie at one point or another, even those "little white lies" count), it's imperative to know the signs that someone may be lying to you. Here are seven of the classic signs to watch out for.

Seven Common Signs of Lying

6　　**1. No eye contact:** Generally, if someone is lying they will not look you in the eye, at least during a certain part of the conversation. Normally, people make eye contact for at least half of a conversation, so anything less than this could be suspicious. One caveat: there are some people who will take great pains to make eye contact with you even if they're lying, simply to make you think they're not.

7　　**2. Change in voice:** A change in the pitch of a person's tone, or a lot of stammering (umm, ah), or throat clearing could indicate a lie.

8　　**3. Unusual body language:** If a person taps their foot a lot, fidgets with their hands, raises their shoulders, turns away from you, or brings their hand to their face (to touch their chin or nose, etc.)—in other words, if they act nervous or uncomfortable—it could mean they're telling a lie. Also watch out for blushing (or becoming pale) and increased blinking.

9　　**4. Something sounds fishy:** Making statements that contradict each other, are inconsistent, or don't sound quite right are usually part of a lie.

10　　**5. Overly defensive:** Sometimes when a person is lying they will become extremely defensive, refusing to answer any questions and even accusing you of lying. This may mean they have something to hide.

11　　**6. Changes subject easily:** If someone is lying and you change the subject, chances are high that they'll go right along with it. A person telling the truth, however, will likely ask why you changed the subject and want to go back to it.

12　　**7. Humor or sarcasm:** A guilty person will often try to change the subject using humor or sarcasm.

13　　Of course, no one behavior can tell for sure whether or not someone is telling the truth or lying. While you should trust your instinct, if you're not sure it's best to try to get some evidence to back up your accusation. Rather than relying on a specific behavior, catching a liar in the act is best done by watching their normal behaviors. When those behaviors suddenly change, that's when a lie has likely been told.

---

1 Gepetto the creator of Pinocchio

Checking Fluency and Comprehension

A. **Which of these are signs of lying? Check (✔) your answers.**

...... 1. No eye contact.

...... 2. Keeping a steady voice.

...... 3. Unusual body language.

...... 4. Changing the subject easily.

...... 5. Seeming too relaxed.

B. **Check your answers with a partner. Record your score on page 193.**

Expanding Vocabulary

A. **Antonyms are words with the opposite meaning. Look in the passage to find antonyms of the words below.**

1. kindly .... (par. 3)

2. healthy .... (par. 4)

3. unimportant .... (par. 5)

4. agree with .... (par. 9)

5. offensive .... (par. 10)

6. innocent .... (par. 12)

B. **Complete the sentences with the antonyms from A. Be sure to use the correct forms.**

1. If I say 'yes,' Jill always says 'no'—she loves to _____ me.

2. Nobody is attacking you, so there's no need to get _____!

3. The criminal left the court a free man after the judge said he was not _____.

4. If a child is injured, it is _____ that we contact the parents.

5. A _____ liar is someone with a diseased mind who cannot tell the truth.

6. Some teenagers _____ threw a brick through the elderly lady's window.

What's Your Opinion?

A. **Do you agree or disagree with these statements? Check (✔) your answers.**

	Agree	Disagree	Not Sure
1. If a friend lied to me, I would end the friendship.	☐	☐	☐
2. You can't really succeed in life without lying.	☐	☐	☐
3. You should never lie to little children.	☐	☐	☐
4. Children lie more than adults.	☐	☐	☐
5. Nearly all advertisements contain lies.	☐	☐	☐

B. **Discuss your answers with a partner. Give reasons for your answers.**

Increasing Fluency

Follow the instructions to practice increasing your reading speed.

1. Look back at your reading time for "The Top Seven Signs that Someone is Lying to You." Write the time here: _____

2. Use a watch to time yourself. Read the text again. Try to read it faster than the first time. Write your new reading time here: _____

3. Did your reading speed increase?

Extensive Reading 3

The Railway Children

Introduction

This extract from an Oxford *Bookworms* reader gives you the opportunity to read more in English. The more you read, the faster and more fluent you will become. *The Railway Children* is set in England. It tells the story of three children growing up: Roberta, Peter, and Phyllis. The extract you will read starts at a happy time before their lives are unexpectedly changed one day.

Before Reading

A. What do you think will happen in the extract? Check (✔) your answers.

.... 1. The children's parents get a divorce.

.... 2. Their father disappears.

.... 3. They move from their nice house in London to a small house in the country.

.... 4. Their mother runs away.

B. Now read the extract to see what happens.

🎧 *CD 1 Track 10*

Words

Mother was almost always at home, ready to play with the children, or to read to them. And she wrote stories, then read them to the children after tea.

These three lucky children had everything that they needed. Pretty clothes, a warm house, and lots of toys. They also had a wonderful father who was never angry and always ready to play a game.　　　　　　　　　　　50

They were very happy. But they did not know *how* happy until their life in London was over, and they had to live a very different life indeed.

The awful change came suddenly.

It was Peter's birthday, and he was ten years old. Among　　100
his presents was a toy steam engine, and it quickly became

Peter's favorite toy. But after three days, the engine went BANG! Peter was very unhappy about his broken toy. The others said he cried, but Peter said his eyes were red because he had a cold.

When Father came home that day, Peter told him the sad story about his engine, and Father looked at it very carefully. Mother and the children waited.

"Is there no hope?" said Peter.

"Of course there's hope!" said Father, smiling. "I'll fix it on Saturday, and you can all help me."

Just then, someone knocked at the front door. A few moments later, Ruth—the maid—came in. "There are two gentlemen to see you," she said to Father.

"Now, who can they be?" said Father.

"Try to be quick, dear," said his wife. "It's nearly time for the children to go to bed."

But the two men stayed and stayed. Father's voice got louder and louder in the next room, but the children and Mother could not hear what was said. Then Ruth came back and spoke to Mother.

"He wants you to go in, ma'am," she said. "I think he's had bad news. Be ready for the worst."

Mother went into the next room, and there was more talking. Soon after, the children heard Ruth call a taxi, then there was the sound of feet going outside and down the steps.

Mother came back, and her face was white.

"It's time to go to bed," she said to the children. "Ruth will take you upstairs."

"But, Father—" began Phyllis.

"Father's had to go away on business," said Mother. "Now, go to bed, darlings."

Bobbie whispered, "It wasn't bad news, was it?"

"No, darling," said Mother. "I can't tell you anything tonight. Please go *now*."

Mother went out early the next morning, and it was nearly seven o'clock before she came home. She looked ill and tired, and the children asked her no questions.

Mother drank a cup of tea, then she said, "Now, my darlings, I want to tell you something. Those men did bring bad news last night. Father will be away for some time, and I'm very worried."

"Is it something to do with the government?" asked Bobbie. The children knew that Father worked in a government office.

"Yes," said Mother. "Now don't ask me any more questions about it. Will you promise me that?"

The children promised.

Everything was horrible for some weeks. Mother was nearly always out. Ruth, the maid, went away. Then Mother went to bed for two days, and the children wondered if the world was coming to an end.

One morning, Mother came down to breakfast. Her face was very white, but she tried to smile.

"We have to leave our house in London," she said. "We're going to live in the country, in a dear little white house near a railway line. I know you'll love it."

A busy week followed, packing everything up in boxes. The children almost enjoyed the excitement.

"We can't take everything," Mother told them. "Just the necessary things. We have to play 'being poor' for a while."

On their last night in the house, Peter had to sleep on the floor, which he enjoyed very much. "I like moving," he said.

"I don't!" said Mother, laughing.

Bobbie saw her face when she turned away. "Oh, Mother," she thought. "How brave you are! How I love you!"

Next day, they went to the railway station, and got on a train. At first, they enjoyed looking out of the windows, but then they became sleepy. Later, Mother woke them.

"Wake up, dears," she said. "We're there."

There were no taxis, and a man with a cart took their boxes. The children and Mother walked behind the cart along a dark, dirty road, which seemed to go across the fields. After a while, a shape appeared in the darkness.

"There's the house," said Mother.

The cart went along by the garden wall, and around to the back door. There were no lights in any of the windows.

"Where's Mrs. Viney?" said Mother.

"Who's she?" asked Bobbie.

"A woman from the village. I asked her to clean the place and make our dinner," said Mother.

"Your train was late," said the man with the cart. "She's probably gone home."

"But she has the key," said Mother.

"It'll be under the doorstep," said the man. He went to look. "Yes, here it is."

They went inside the dark house. There was a large kitchen with a stone floor, but there was no fire, and the room was cold. There was a candle on the table, and the man lit it. Then a noise seemed to come from inside the walls of the house. It sounded like small animals running up and down. Then the cart man went away and shut the door. Immediately, the candle went out.

"Oh, I wish we hadn't come!" said Phyllis.

Extract from *The Railway Children*, Bookworms Library, Oxford University Press.

Total Words: 941

After Reading

Answer the questions.

1. Why are the children happy at the beginning of the story?

   ....

2. What happened to the children's father?

   ....

3. What is the house in the country near to?

   ....

4. Why didn't the mother tell the children the truth? Why did she lie to them about their father?

   ....

Thinking About the Story

Answer the questions.

1. Did you enjoy reading the extract? Do you want to read more about Roberta, Peter, and Phyllis?
2. Do you think their father is a criminal?
3. Why do you think the book is entitled *The Railway Children*?

Timed Repeated Reading

How many words can you read in one minute? Follow the instructions to practice increasing your reading speed.

1. Time yourself. Read the extract for one minute. When you stop, underline the last word you read and write "first" in the margin.
2. Go back to the beginning of the extract. Read again for one minute. Try to read faster this time. When you stop, underline the last word you read and write "second" in the margin.
3. Go back to the beginning of the extract. Read again for one minute. Try to read even faster this time. When you stop, underline the last word you read and write "third" in the margin.
4. Count the number of words you read each time. Record the three numbers on the Timed Repeated Reading Chart on page 193.

Unit 4

Hoaxes

Discuss the questions.

1. Look at the photo. Do you think it's real?
2. What are some ways people try to fool the public?

This unit is about hoaxes. A hoax is a plan to deceive someone. Sometimes it is a joke. Sometimes it is more serious. In Part 1, you will read about April Fool's Day hoaxes. In Part 2, you will read about hoaxes on the Internet. The unit is followed by Extensive Reading 4, which is an extract from a book called *Skyjack!* It is the story, full of deception and danger, of an attempt by three terrorists to hijack an airplane.

Before Reading

Discuss the questions.

1. What is April Fool's Day?
2. What kinds of tricks are fun to play on other people?

Comprehension Strategy: Distinguishing Fact from Opinion

It is important to know the difference between *facts* and *opinions*. You can check a fact to see if it is true or false. Opinions are feelings or beliefs; they cannot be checked. Words such as *feel, think, believe,* and *should* often indicate opinions.

A. Find the sentences in the text. Mark them as fact (F) or opinion (O).

........**a.** The article was published on April 1, but some readers were taken in by the hoax.

........**b.** The best jokes should make everyone laugh, even the person on whom the joke is played.

........**c.** The British Broadcasting Company (BBC) is famous for its April 1 hoaxes.

........**d.** In a world full of wars and problems, I believe it is fun to take a break and play tricks on one another once a year.

B. Read the entire text and answer the questions that follow.

🎧 *CD 1 Track 11*

Hoaxes and April Fool's Day

1   The news was astounding: According to a Singapore newspaper, *The Straits Times*, the Singapore Zoo had plans to show a pair of highly intelligent apes, known as *simia mina*. These apes are close relatives of gorillas and chimpanzees and, according to the article, talk to one another, use tools, and walk upright, just like humans. The article was published on April 1, but some readers were taken in by the hoax.

2   April Fool's Day is one of the funniest and most popular traditions enjoyed by people everywhere. In France, April 1 is called *Poisson d'Avril*, which means April Fish. Children delight in sticking paper fish to their friends' backs and shouting "Poisson d'Avril." In England, you can only play tricks in the morning. When someone tricks you, you are a "noodle." In Scotland, when you are tricked, you are called an "April gowk," or a cuckoo bird.

3   There are a number of stories about the source of April Fool's Day. One of the most widely believed stories concerns the introduction of a new calendar in Europe. In 1582, France became the first country to switch from the Julian calendar to the Gregorian calendar, the one widely used today. This new calendar changed the beginning of the new year from the end of March to January 1. Some people either didn't know about the new calendar, or they ignored it and continued to observe the beginning of the new year on April 1. Those who had changed and celebrated the new year on January 1 called them April fools and played tricks on them.

4   April Fool's practical jokes should be funny and not hurt other people. The best jokes should make everyone laugh, even the person on whom the joke is played. Good examples of funny, harmless tricks are putting food coloring in milk and gluing a coin to the sidewalk.

5   *The Straits Times* is not the only print medium to play hoaxes. The magazine *Discover* announced in its April 1995 issue that Dr. Aprile Pazzo, a well-known wildlife biologist, had discovered a new species in Antarctica: the hotheaded naked ice borer. These incredible creatures had bony plates on their heads that became extremely hot. These hot bony plates allowed the naked ice borers to drill through ice at high speeds. This helped the animals to hunt penguins by melting the ice underneath the penguins. The hot ice melted, and the penguins would sink into the slush[1] where the hotheads ate them.

6   The British Broadcasting Company (BBC) is famous for its April 1 hoaxes. In 1957, the BBC showed a video of Swiss farmers pulling strands of spaghetti from their trees. The newscaster said the mild winter had resulted in a huge crop of spaghetti. Some viewers believed the report and called the BBC to find out how they could grow their own spaghetti trees.

spaghetti trees

7   One clever BBC hoax was a report on the discovery of a new species of night-singing tree mice known as musendrophilus. A group of scientists claimed they discovered the night-singing tree mice on the Sheba Islands in the Pacific Ocean. To make the hoax even more believable, fake recordings of the sounds of the night-singing tree mice were played for the audience. The listening audience was also told that the Sheba islanders used the webbed feet of the animal to help them make music.

8   In a world full of wars and problems, I believe it is fun to take a break and play tricks on one another once a year. Let's hope that we never lose this wonderful and delightful tradition.

1 **slush** very soft ice mixed with water

Checking Comprehension

A. These sentences are false. Correct the facts.

1. In England, you can only play tricks on April 1 in the afternoon.

   ....

2. In 1582, France became the first country to switch from the Gregorian to the Julian Calendar.

   ....

3. Putting food coloring in milk and gluing a coin to the sidewalk are examples of mean and nasty tricks.

   ....

4. Nobody believed the BBC's report about the spaghetti trees.

   ....

5. The BBC played real recordings of the night-singing tree mice for the audience.

   ....

6. The author hopes that we lose the tradition of April Fool's Day.

   ....

B. Match the expressions from the text with their definition.

........1. Poisson D'Avril   **a.** someone tricked in England on April 1

........2. noodle   **b.** April fish

........3. April gowk   **c.** imaginary talking ape

........4. musendrophilus   **d.** someone tricked in Scotland on April 1

........5. simia mina   **e.** imaginary singing tree mouse

Looking at Vocabulary in Context

A. Find the words in bold in the text. Circle the words that complete the sentences.

1. The *shocking information / boring truth* was **astounding**. (par. 1)

2. *Unlike / Like* horses, humans walk **upright**. (par. 1)

3. Mariko believes *everything / nothing* she reads on the Web, so she was **taken in by** (par. 1) the hoax.

4. Greedy people **delight in** (par. 2) *getting things / giving things away*.

5. A **biologist** (par. 5) studies *rocks and minerals / animals and plants*.

6. When people **take a break** (par. 8), they *relax / work harder*.

B. Fill in the blanks with the words in bold from A. Be sure to use the correct forms.

1. She _____ baking fresh bread for her family.

2. Because Sang-ki loves wildlife, he is studying to be a _____.

3. Even though John had been told about the hoax, he was still _____ it.

4. After studying for three hours, they decided to _____.

5. The audience thought the magician's tricks were _____.

6. With training, a horse can learn to walk _____ on two legs.

What's Your Opinion?

Discuss the questions.

1. Are you the kind of person who enjoys playing tricks on other people?

2. Do you mind having tricks played on you?

3. How can playing tricks be dangerous?

4. What television shows feature playing tricks on people?

5. Is it OK for the news media to play tricks on the public?

Internet Hoaxes

Before Reading

Are the statements true or false?

1. Do you believe everything you read on the Internet?
2. Do you use the Internet to send jokes to your friends?

Fluency Strategy: Ignoring Unknown Words

You don't need to know the meaning of every word to understand the meaning of a text. Put your dictionary away. When you come to words you don't know, ignore them. Keep reading. Think about what you can understand—not what you can't—to increase your reading fluency.

A. Use the strategy to read the text. Mark these statements true (T), false (F), or don't know (?).

........**1.** Wipe Out is not really a dangerous virus.

........**2.** The author forwarded the virus warning to many people.

........**3.** Snowball was a normal cat.

........**4.** The author enjoys playing hoaxes on the Internet.

B. Read the whole text quickly again. Record your reading time below and on the chart on page 193.

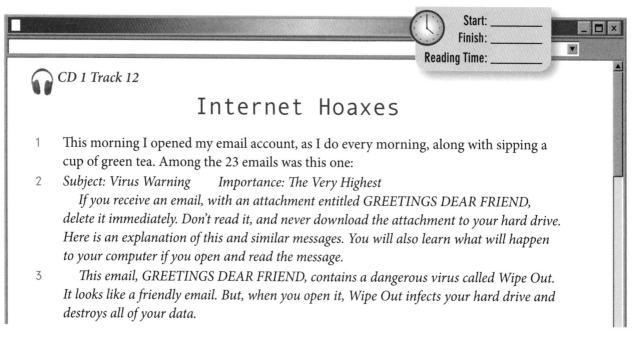

Start: _____
Finish: _____
Reading Time: _____

CD 1 Track 12

Internet Hoaxes

1   This morning I opened my email account, as I do every morning, along with sipping a cup of green tea. Among the 23 emails was this one:

2   *Subject: Virus Warning   Importance: The Very Highest*
     If you receive an email, with an attachment entitled GREETINGS DEAR FRIEND, delete it immediately. Don't read it, and never download the attachment to your hard drive. Here is an explanation of this and similar messages. You will also learn what will happen to your computer if you open and read the message.

3   *This email, GREETINGS DEAR FRIEND, contains a dangerous virus called Wipe Out. It looks like a friendly email. But, when you open it, Wipe Out infects your hard drive and destroys all of your data.*

4   *Furthermore, it doesn't stop with your hard drive. Wipe Out reproduces itself. When you open it, it automatically forwards itself to all of the addresses in your email address file.*

5   *In addition to destroying all data on your computer's hard drive, Wipe Out destroys the data on the hard drives of the people whose emails are in your inbox. Even worse, it will destroy the data on the hard drives of the people whose emails are in everyone else's inboxes!*

6   *We must stop this terrible, destructive virus. Think of the damage that Wipe Out can do. If we fail to stop it, Wipe Out will destroy computer networks all over the world because it reproduces itself. Again, remember, if you receive an email entitled GREETINGS DEAR FRIEND, delete it! Don't hesitate. Help kill Wipe Out!*

7   *Forward this email to everyone whose email address you have. It will also be helpful if you could forward it to any newsgroups and mailing lists you are on. Please join in the worldwide campaign to wipe out Wipe Out!*

8   To tell the truth, I was nervous after reading this email. I read it carefully again. I thought about forwarding it to several newsgroups to which I belong. I figured it might forestall the spread of Wipe Out. But then, I had second thoughts. I wondered if it was another Internet hoax. So, I did some serious research and learned that it was a harmless hoax. When we get this kind of an email, it will not hurt our computers. But, it does waste our time.

9   I did some more research and learned some more about Internet hoaxes. One of the most famous was about a cat named Snowball. A picture of a man holding a huge cat appeared on the Internet in 2000. The cat was as big as a large dog.

10   The photograph was sent all over the world, with no explanation about the cat or the man. But someone, nobody knows who, wrote a short explanation. According to this explanation, Snowball is owned by Rodger Degagne, who lives in Canada. Mr. Degagne found Snowball's mother near a Canadian nuclear laboratory. Mr. Degagne took the cat home with him. A short time later, the cat gave birth to Snowball, who quickly grew into a monster-size cat weighing 39.5 kilograms.

11   However, both the story and the photograph were fake. Cordell Hauglie, an American, said that "Snowball" was his daughter's cat. The cat, named Jumper, only weighed 9.5 kilograms. Mr. Hauglie said that he made the fake photograph and then emailed it to several friends. He did this as a joke and did not even think about making an Internet hoax. It took only two months for the photograph to spread around the world.

12   I had an interesting time surfing the Internet to learn about hoaxes. But I did waste a lot of time!

Checking Fluency and Comprehension

A. Complete the sentences. Do not look back at the text.

1. The email described Wipe Out as ....
   a. a harmless Internet hoax.
   b. a destructive computer virus.

2. After receiving the email about Wipe Out, the author ....
   a. forwarded it to several newsgroups.
   b. did some research on the Internet.

3. According to the author, email hoaxes ....
   a. cost a great deal of money.
   b. waste our time.

4. Snowball was a cat that was ....
   a. part of a famous Internet hoax.
   b. proven to be as big as a dog.

5. Mr. Hauglie made the fake photograph ....
   a. as an April Fool's Internet hoax.
   b. as a joke for a few friends.

B. Check your answers with a partner. Record your score on page 193.

Expanding Vocabulary

A. Compound words are made up of two smaller words. Look in the text to find compound words. Match them with the definitions.

1. .... (par. 2)—take from the Internet and put in your own computer

2. .... (par. 5)—the place where new email is kept

3. .... (par. 6)—interconnected groups of computers

4. .... (par. 7)—a place to share informational messages on a certain subject

5. .... (par. 7)—all over the earth

6. .... (par. 8)—block the progress of something

B. Fill in the blanks with the compound words from A. Be sure to use the correct forms.

1. I belong to a/an _____ about gardening—I get lots of interesting information from the other members.

2. I had 75 emails in my _____ this morning.

3. Instead of buying CDs, I just _____ all the music I wanted from the Internet.

4. The army was unable to _____ the advance of the enemy soldiers.

5. At the end of the 20th century, fast food restaurants became very popular _____ .

6. Most large companies connect all their computers in a/an _____ to improve efficiency.

What's Your Opinion?

Discuss the questions.

1. Do you think that viruses are a serious problem on the Internet?
2. What do you do to protect your computer from viruses?
3. What do you do to stop unwanted email?
4. Have you or anyone you know been the victim of an Internet hoax?
5. Do you open every email you get, or do you throw some away unopened?

Increasing Fluency

Read the paragraph quickly; don't stop to think about the missing words. Mark the statements below true (T) or false (F).

Chain Letters

Chain letters are similar to Internet hoaxes. They are email XXXXX that ask you to do something. The creators of chain XXXXX want you to forward them to everyone you know. Chain letters promise you money or even XXXXX luck when you forward them. They also warn you of bad luck if you fail to send them to XXXXX you know. The chain letters that promise money appeal to people's greed.

_____ 1. A chain letter requires some action of the person who receives it.

_____ 2. The purpose of chain letters is to sell you something.

_____ 3. Some people forward chain letters because they are greedy.

Extensive Reading 4

Skyjack!

Skyjack!

Introduction

This extract from an Oxford *Bookworms* reader gives you the opportunity to read more in English. The more you read, the faster and more fluent you will become. *Skyjack!* is set aboard an airplane that is being hijacked by three terrorists. The extract you will read starts as two people, Carl and Harald, are boarding the plane.

Before Reading

A. What do you think you will find out in the extract? Check (✔) your answers.

......1. Carl and Harald are two of the terrorists who hijack the airplane.

......2. A flight attendant helps the terrorists.

......3. Carl is a policeman and tries to stop the terrorists.

......4. The terrorists kill Harald.

B. Now read the extract to see what happens.

🎧 *CD 1 Track 13*

Words

The flight attendant smiled. "Welcome aboard, sir. Would you like a newspaper?"

"Yes, please." Carl took the newspaper and looked at his ticket. "I'm in seat 5F. Where's that?"

"It's near the front of the plane, sir. On the left, there. By the window."

"I see. Thank you very much." Carl smiled back at the flight attendant. She was young and pretty. Just like my daughter, he thought.   50

He put his bag under his seat and sat down. His friend Harald sat beside him. They watched the other passengers coming onto the plane. Harald looked at his watch.

"9:30 P.M.," he said. "Good. We're on time."   100

Carl agreed. "And in three hours we'll be home," he said. "That's good. We've been away for a long time. You'll be pleased to see your family, won't you, Harald?"

Harald smiled. "Yes, I will. Have you seen this, sir?" He opened his bag and took out two small planes. "These are for my sons. I always bring something back for them."

"How old are your sons?" Carl asked.

"Five and almost seven. The older one has a birthday tomorrow."

"He'll be very excited tonight then."

"Yes. I hope he gets some sleep."

The plane took off. Carl watched the lights of the airport grow smaller below them. Then the plane flew above the clouds and he could see the moon and the stars in the night sky. He lay back in his seat and closed his eyes.

* * *

Later, he woke up. Harald was asleep. Carl looked at his watch. It was midnight. He called the flight attendant.

"Excuse me. What time do we arrive?"

"11:30 P.M. local time, sir. That's about half an hour from now."

"Thank you." Carl changed the time on his watch.

"Anything else, sir?"

"No, I don't think so. Oh, wait a minute—could I have a cup of coffee, please?"

"Yes, of course, sir." He watched her bring the coffee. "She walks like my daughter, too," he thought. "And she is *very* young. She looks nervous, not sure what to do."

"How long have you been a flight attendant?" he asked.

She smiled. "Three months, sir," she said.

"Do you like it?"

"Yes, I love it. It's very exciting." She smiled nervously. "Will that be all, sir?"

"Yes, thank you."

"Have a nice flight."

He drank the coffee and started to read his newspaper. When Harald woke up, Carl showed him a page in the paper.

"Look. There you are," he said. He pointed to a picture. In the middle of the picture stood Carl himself—a short thin man with gray hair, wearing a suit. Behind him, on the left, was Harald—a tall, strong young man, like an athlete. Both men were smiling. "That's you and me, outside the Embassy," said Carl. "We're in the news again. You can show it to your sons. You're a famous man, Harald!"

Harald laughed. "You're the famous man, sir, not me," he said. "I'm just a police officer. It's my job to take care of you. That's a photo of you, not me."

"Perhaps. But your children think that you're a famous man, I'm sure. Here, take it, and show it to them."

"OK. Thanks." Harald smiled, and put the newspaper in his coat pocket. "I think I'll have a cup of coffee too." He called for the flight attendant, but she did not come. Harald looked surprised.

"What's the matter?" Carl asked.

"The flight attendant," Harald said. "She's sitting down talking to those two men."

Carl looked up and saw the young flight attendant. She was sitting in a seat at the front of the plane with two young men. They looked worried and nervous. Suddenly, one of the young men picked up a bag and *walked into the pilot's cabin*! The other man and the flight attendant followed him.

"That's strange," said Carl. "What are they doing?"

"I don't know. It's very strange," said Harald. "I don't like it at all." He began to get out of his seat, but then stopped and sat down again.

For one or two minutes nothing happened. None of the other passengers moved or spoke. They had seen the young men, too. It became very quiet in the plane.

A bell rang, and for a moment they could hear two voices arguing. Then the pilot spoke.

"Ladies and gentlemen, this is the Captain speaking. Please do not be afraid. There is a change of plan. We have to land at another airport before we finish our journey. There's no danger. We will land in fifteen minutes. Please stay in your seats and keep calm. Thank you."

Then the flight attendant came out of the cabin. She looked very different now because she had a machine gun in her hand. She stood at the front of the plane and watched the passengers carefully.

Extract from *Skyjack!*, Bookworms Library, Oxford University Press.

After Reading

Answer the questions.

1. Who did Harald buy gifts for?

   ....

2. Why did the flight attendant seem nervous?

   ....

3. Why did the flight attendant talk with the two men?

   ....

4. Which of the two men, Harald or Carl, is very important?

   ....

Thinking About the Story

Answer the questions.

1. Did you enjoy reading the extract? Do you want to read more about the hijacking?
2. What is Harald's job?
3. What do you think will happen to the passengers on the airplane?

Timed Repeated Reading

How many words can you read in one minute? Follow the instructions to practice increasing your reading speed.

1. Time yourself. Read the extract for one minute. When you stop, underline the last word you read and write "first" in the margin.
2. Go back to the beginning of the extract. Read again for one minute. Try to read faster this time. When you stop, underline the last word you read and write "second" in the margin.
3. Go back to the beginning of the extract. Read again for one minute. Try to read even faster this time. When you stop, underline the last word you read and write "third" in the margin.
4. Count the number of words you read each time. Record the three numbers on the Timed Repeated Reading Chart on page 193.

Unit 5

The Sea

Discuss the questions.

1. When did you last visit the sea? What did you do there?
2. Do you enjoy water sports? Which ones do you like?

This unit is about the sea. In Part 1, you will read a newspaper article about two boys who were lost at sea. In Part 2, you will read about a brave surfer girl who survived a shark attack. The unit is followed by Extensive Reading 2, which is an extract from a book called *Kidnapped*. It is a story about a young man from Scotland who is kidnapped and taken away to sea.

Part 1   Lost at Sea

Before Reading

Discuss the questions.

1. How could a person become lost at sea?
2. What kinds of problems would a person lost at sea in a small boat encounter?

Comprehension Strategy: Identifying Meaning from Context

You can often guess the meaning of words you don't know from the context. Think about the topic. Look at sentences before and after the word. They may give clues such as examples, contrasts, or synonyms that help identify the unknown word.

A. Find the words in bold in the text. Use the strategy to work out the meanings, then circle the answers.

1. **Drizzled** (par. 5) probably means *rained lightly* / *rained heavily.*
2. **Hail** (par. 8) probably means *signal* / *ride.*
3. **Blustery** (par. 11) probably means *sunny* / *windy.*

B. Read the whole text and answer the questions that follow.

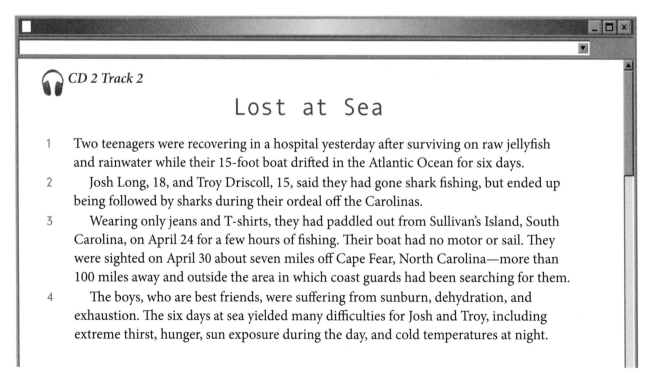

CD 2 Track 2

Lost at Sea

1   Two teenagers were recovering in a hospital yesterday after surviving on raw jellyfish and rainwater while their 15-foot boat drifted in the Atlantic Ocean for six days.

2   Josh Long, 18, and Troy Driscoll, 15, said they had gone shark fishing, but ended up being followed by sharks during their ordeal off the Carolinas.

3   Wearing only jeans and T-shirts, they had paddled out from Sullivan's Island, South Carolina, on April 24 for a few hours of fishing. Their boat had no motor or sail. They were sighted on April 30 about seven miles off Cape Fear, North Carolina—more than 100 miles away and outside the area in which coast guards had been searching for them.

4   The boys, who are best friends, were suffering from sunburn, dehydration, and exhaustion. The six days at sea yielded many difficulties for Josh and Troy, including extreme thirst, hunger, sun exposure during the day, and cold temperatures at night.

5   Josh said, "We gargled with seawater and spat it out. It drizzled one night and we licked water off the deck, trying to get *something* in us. That's all we had."

6   During the day they took dips in the water to cool off under the midday sun, but they soon discovered that sharks were swimming under the boat. Josh said he had always tried to keep in mind his father's advice that sharks were just curious.

7   But he added, "When we were swimming around they would come up and start swimming toward us. That's when we got out of there. Every time we would get in the water, there was one coming."

8   Attempts to hail passing ships failed. One night they were awakened by splashing waves to find a large freight ship coming quickly toward them. The huge ship came within feet of their boat, and the wave from the ship almost capsized[1] them.

9   "It was like a monster building in the water," Troy said. "It sounded like a hurricane. That's when we thought we were going to die."

10   They kept up their spirits by singing and dreaming of milk shakes and ice cream. Josh said, "You could see nothing but miles of ocean. We just prayed every day. We prayed for our families, prayed for our lives, prayed to get home. God answered us."

11   The boys had set out on a blustery day despite a warning from the National Weather Service that small boats should stay off the water. They realized they were in trouble almost immediately and thought of trying to swim ashore, pulling the boat with them. But Josh remembered his grandfather's advice that you should always stay with your boat, and decided against swimming. Within hours, they were far out to sea.

12   They lost their fishing tackle on the second day, so they had no way to catch fish. That's when Troy resorted to eating jellyfish. "After several days, I knew I had to eat something," he said. "It smelled really nasty. It was like a little jelly ball. I just slurped them down." But Josh refused to eat them, fearing they would make him sick.

13   At night, when it became cold, they shared a single wetsuit to try to keep warm—one wore the top, and the other wore the bottom. They held each other tight under a shelf on the front of the boat. "I was freezing cold," Troy said. "Half our bodies were lying in water."

14   Eddie Long, Josh's father, said, "The coast guard was telling us to expect bodies to float up in between seven to ten days. But we knew there was room for a miracle, and this is our miracle."

---

1 capsize turn upside down in the water

Checking Comprehension

Answer the questions.

1. What was the author's purpose in writing this article?
   a. To warn boaters about the bad weather conditions.
   b. To inform readers about the boys' survival story at sea.
   c. To educate readers about how they can survive at sea.

2. Why did Josh and Troy go out to sea that day?
   a. To fish for sharks.
   b. To get to a small island.
   c. To enjoy swimming in the sea.

3. How did the boys get lost at sea?
   a. The weather was poor and very windy.
   b. The boys did not know how to paddle well.
   c. The boys could not paddle back because of sharks.

4. How did the boys keep warm at night?
   a. They used blankets and held each other.
   b. The water in the boat kept them warm.
   c. They shared a wetsuit and held each other.

5. Which of the following difficulties did the boys NOT experience?
   a. A shark bite.
   b. Not enough drinking water.
   c. Too much sun exposure.

6. When did the boys think they were going to die?
   a. When a large ship almost hit them.
   b. When they got sick from eating jellyfish.
   c. When they got chased by sharks.

Looking at Vocabulary in Context

A. Find the words in bold in the text. Match the words with the definitions.

...... 1. **recovering** (par. 1)   **a.** painful or difficult experience

...... 2. **ordeal** (par. 2)   **b.** loss of water

...... 3. **dehydration** (par. 4)   **c.** very bad

...... 4. **yielded** (par. 4)   **d.** produced or created

...... 5. **keep in mind** (par. 6)   **e.** getting better

...... 6. **nasty** (par. 12)   **f.** remember or think about

B. Fill in the blanks with the words from A. Be sure to use the correct forms.

1. After walking in the hot sun for hours, I began to feel the effects of ....

2. Although final exam scores are important, students should .... that class participation is also a part of their grade.

3. It will take many people a long time to .... from the damage caused by the earthquake.

4. The shocking .... left Sue with no home and very little money.

5. The experiment .... many positive results.

6. My neighbors never take out their trash, so the smell is quite ....

What's Your Opinion?

A. Imagine you are lost at sea on a small boat with a friend. Write three things you want to have with you, and your reason, in the chart.

Item	Reason
1.	
2.	
3.	

B. Discuss your answers with a partner.

Before Reading

Answer the questions.

1. Are you afraid of sharks?
2. What would you do if you met a shark?

Fluency Strategy: Previewing and Predicting

> Previewing means looking at the text title and images (photos, graphs, etc.) before you start reading. After previewing, you should try to predict what the text will be about. Previewing and predicting before you start reading can help you improve your understanding of the text when you read.

A. Use the strategy to predict the topic of the text. Circle your answer.

1. The tragic death of a young surfer who was attacked by a shark.
2. The dangers of surfing and how to avoid shark attacks.
3. A surfer who, after having been attacked by a shark, became famous.

B. Read the whole text quickly. Record your reading time below and on the chart on page 193.

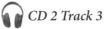 CD 2 Track 3

Start: _____
Finish: _____
Reading Time: _____

From Surfer to Celebrity

1   In 2003, Bethany Hamilton, a 13-year-old competitive surfer, was attacked by a 14-foot tiger shark while surfing off the coast of Hawaii. She was on her surfboard resting in the water when the shark attacked her by surprise. In the struggle, the shark ripped off her left arm.

2   Instead of panicking, Bethany was able to paddle over to her friends, who quickly helped her to shore. Along the way, Bethany remained strong, and even shouted to other surfers to warn them about the shark. Once on the shore, her friend's father used a surfboard rope to tie around Bethany's shoulder and help slow the bleeding—the doctors say that this probably saved her life.

3   Although Bethany lost her arm, she refused to let the traumatic shark attack end her dream of becoming a surfer. After her recovery, she got back in the water and on her surfboard. In order to make up for the loss of her arm, she says she needs to kick a lot harder. Even so, she still loves surfing as much as ever.

4   Understandably, Bethany is also more cautious when it comes to sharks. She's painted a special pattern on her surfboard that looks like a poisonous sea snake, which helps to scare away sharks. As an extra precaution, she avoids surfing during the early morning and dusk[1] hours, which are sharks' favorite feeding times.

5   Bethany also hasn't lost her competitive spirit. She continues to train regularly, and is competing and succeeding in surf competitions once again. In fact, since the attack, she's won three surfing competitions and an award for Best Comeback[2] Athlete.

6   By now, people all over the world have heard of her story. She is recognized as a brave and tenacious hero. In an effort to help and inspire others, Bethany has chosen to use her new celebrity status for charitable causes. For example, in her home state of Hawaii, she has appeared in anti-drug ads in the hopes of keeping young people off drugs. Also, after the massive tsunami in 2004, she visited Thailand to help children hurt by the disaster. Simon, from kidzworld.com, was able to catch up with Bethany and ask her a few questions:

7   *What was the hardest thing about recovering from your injury?*
Getting back on the surfboard after the attack was the hardest thing, and I did it! After that, the hardest thing was my first competition, but I'm now ranked fourth in the world in under-18 women.

8   *What sort of things do you miss doing since your injury?*
I don't really miss anything. I've never had more to do. I'm traveling and meeting influential people from around the world. The only thing I miss a little is playing the ukulele.

9   *How do you deal with all the publicity you've had since the attack?*
Every day I just balance life with my surfing, my friends, and my new public career. When I have a public engagement it is all about the message—*believe in your dreams.*

10   *What are your favorite sports other than surfing?*
I love playing soccer—that means a lot to me. I love the teamwork and the running.

11   *What are your future surfing plans?*
I'd like to be surfing on the pro circuit[3] in three years, and I should be ready. I'd also like to continue to write inspirational books. My new book is a best seller, and my movie will be a popular story too. Most of all, I want to do something good for kids—like the kids in Thailand who were affected by the tsunami disaster, who I've been helping to take back into the water.

Bethany Hamilton

1 dusk the time in the evening just before it becomes dark
2 comeback become successful again
3 pro circuit professional-level competitions

Checking Fluency and Comprehension

A. Mark these statements true (T) or false (F). Do not look back at the text.

........1. Bethany was able to remain calm after being attacked by the shark.

........2. Bethany still enjoys surfing anytime during the day.

........3. Since the attack, Bethany has won several surfing competitions.

........4. There are many things that Bethany misses since the loss of her arm.

........5. Bethany is worried that she cannot become a professional surfer.

B. Check your answers with a partner. Record your score on page 193.

Expanding Vocabulary

A. Find other forms of these words in the text. Write the part of speech.

	Word in text	Part of speech
1. trauma (noun)	.... (par. 3)	....
2. caution (noun)	.... (par. 4)	....
3. tenacity (noun)	.... (par. 6)	....
4. mass (noun)	.... (par. 6)	....
5. public (adjective)	.... (par. 9)	....
6. engage (verb)	.... (par. 9)	....

B. Fill in the blanks with the correct form of the words from A.

1. Great white sharks are truly _____ in size, regularly reaching lengths of over six meters.

2. Being attacked by a shark is a/an _____ experience.

3. The _____ dog never gave up fighting the much larger bear.

4. Please excuse me, I have a/an _____ at 6:00 that I can't be late for.

5. The actress went on several talk shows to get _____ for her new movie.

6. When walking on the beach, be _____; there's broken glass in the sand.

What's Your Opinion?

Discuss the questions.

1. How would your life change if you lost an arm?

2. Have you heard Bethany's story before? What was your reaction?

3. In English there is a saying: "If you fall off the horse, you need to get back on it and ride again!" In Bethany's case, she got back on her surfboard. Has there been a time in your life when you've had to "get back on the horse"?

4. Bethany's story of bravery is very inspirational. Who are some inspirational people from your own country?

5. Bethany uses her fame to help other people. Do you know any famous charitable people from your own country who have helped other people?

Increasing Fluency

Scan the line to find the phrase on the left. Phrases may appear more than once. Can you finish in 15 seconds?

	a	b	c	d	e
1. keep up	keep out	keep up	keep down	keep off	keep away
2. once again	once more	one try	try again	once again	one more
3. give up	give up	pick up	give out	give in	give up
4. rip off	rip up	rig up	rid of	rip off	ride out
5. scare away	scare away	shoo away	scare off	take away	send away
6. make up	take up	make use	make up	make out	make out
7. me first	my first	me first	my fast	me first	me fits
8. now ranked	now ranked	now ranged	not ranked	now cranked	now ranked

Extensive Reading 5

Kidnapped

Introduction

This extract from an Oxford *Bookworms* reader gives you the opportunity to read more in English. The more you read, the faster and more fluent you will become. *Kidnapped*, set in 1751, is the story of a young man from the lowlands of Scotland, David Balfour, who leaves home to begin a new life. He meets his rich uncle, who is very upset to discover he has a poor nephew. His uncle arranges for David to be kidnapped and taken away to sea on a ship. The extract you will read starts after the ship has sunk and David, with the help of a piece of wood, has swum to an island.

Before Reading

A. What do you think will happen in the extract? Check (✔) your answers.

.... **1.** David finds some friends on the island.

.... **2.** Some fishermen tell David how to leave the island.

.... **3.** Wild animals attack David, but he escapes.

.... **4.** David is able to walk from the island to the shores of Scotland.

B. Now read the extract to see what happens.

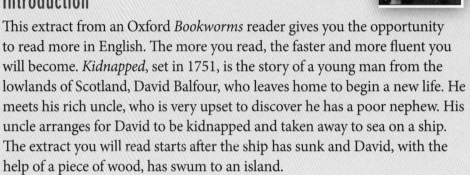 *CD 2 Track 4*

Words

It was a cold night, so I could not sit down to rest. Instead, I walked up and down on the beach, trying to keep warm. There was no sound except the crash of the waves. I felt very lonely and afraid.

In the morning I climbed a hill and looked out over the sea, but there was nothing at all on the water. And around me on the island I could not see any houses or people. I did not like to think what had happened to my friend Alan and the others, and I did not want to look at this emptiness any longer. So I climbed down again, and walked eastward. I was hoping to find a house, where I could dry my clothes and get something to eat.

50

100

I soon discovered that nobody lived on Earraid. It was too far to swim to Mull, which I could see across the water. I thought perhaps I could wade across, but when I tried it, the water was too deep, and I had to turn back. By now it had started to rain, and I felt very miserable.

Then I remembered the piece of wood which had already saved my life once. It would help me to get across the sea to Mull! So I walked all the way back to the beach where I had arrived. The piece of wood was in the sea, so I waded into the water to get it. But as I came closer, it moved away from me. And when the water was too deep for me to stand, the piece of wood was still several

meters away. I had to leave it, and went back to the beach. It was a terrible moment for me. I was feeling very tired, hungry, and thirsty, with no hope of getting away from this lonely island. For the first time since leaving Essendean, I lay down and cried.

300

I do not want to remember the time that I spent on Earraid. I had nothing with me except my uncle's gold and Alan's silver button, and as I had never lived near the sea, I did not know what to eat or how to fish. In fact, I found some shellfish among the rocks on the coast, and ate them, but I was very sick afterward. That was the only food that I could find, so I was always hungry on Earraid. All day and all night it rained heavily, but there was no roof or tree on the island, and my clothes were cold and wet on my body.

350

400

I chose to spend most of my time in the north of Earraid, on a little hill. From here I could see the old church on the island of Iona, not far away to the west, and smoke from people's houses on Mull, to the east. I used to watch this

450

smoke, and think of the people there, and their comfortable lives. This gave me a little hope, in my lonely life among the rocks and the rain and the cold sea.

Two days passed, and on the third day two things happened. First, I discovered that I had lost almost all my money through a hole in my pocket. I only had three of my uncle's thirty-eight pounds left. But worse was to come. While I was sitting on a rock, looking out over Iona, I suddenly noticed a small boat moving fast through the water. I jumped to my feet and shouted as loudly as I could. The two men in the boat were near enough to hear. They shouted back in Gaelic, and laughed. But the boat did not turn, and sailed on, right in front of my eyes, to Iona.

I could not understand why they did not come to help me. I continued shouting wildly, although I could no longer see them. And then, I lay down and cried for the second time. This time I wasn't sad, but angry, because I thought that they had left me to die alone in that terrible place.

The next morning, I was surprised to see that the same men were sailing toward Earraid from Iona. At once I ran down to the rocky coast to meet them. The boat came near me, but stayed a few meters away in the water. There was a third man in the boat, who was talking and laughing with the others. Then he stood up and spoke fast to me in Gaelic, which I could not understand. But sometimes he used an English word, and once I heard the word "tide." This gave me a flash of hope.

"Do you mean—that when the tide is low . . .?" I cried, and could not finish.

"Yes, yes," he called back. "Tide," and laughed again.

I turned my back on the boat and ran back excitedly to the east of the island, where Earraid was closest to Mull. And sure enough, there was now only a little water between the islands. I was able to wade through it easily, and reached Mull with a happy shout. How stupid of me not to realize that it was possible to get to Mull, twice a

850
Total Words: 864

day, at low tide! Now I felt very grateful to the boatmen for guessing my problem, and coming back to help me.

Extract from *Kidnapped*, Bookworms Library, Oxford University Press.

After Reading

Answer the questions.

1. What did David eat when he was on the island?

2. Why was David not able to understand the fishermen at first?

3. Why did David prefer the north part of the island?

4. What did the fishermen tell David to do?

Thinking About the Story

Answer the questions.

1. Did you enjoy reading the extract? Do you want to read more about David and his adventures?
2. Do you think David will see his uncle again?
3. Will David ever return home?

Timed Repeated Reading

How many words can you read in one minute? Follow the instructions to practice increasing your reading speed.

1. Time yourself. Read the extract for one minute. When you stop, underline the last word you read and write "first" in the margin.
2. Go back to the beginning of the extract. Read again for one minute. Try to read faster this time. When you stop, underline the last word you read and write "second" in the margin.
3. Go back to the beginning of the extract. Read again for one minute. Try to read even faster this time. When you stop, underline the last word you read and write "third" in the margin.
4. Count the number of words you read each time. Record the three numbers on the Timed Repeated Reading Chart on page 193.

Unit 6

Learning

Discuss the questions.

1. How much do you remember from your first years of going to school?
2. Do you think that children learn differently than adults?

This unit is about learning. In Part 1, you will read about learning through failure. In Part 2, you will read about memory and learning. The unit is followed by Extensive Reading 6, which is an extract from a short story entitled "Tobermory." It is about a cat that learned how to talk.

Before Reading

Discuss the questions.

1. Have you ever done poorly on a test? How did you feel?
2. Why might someone hope that another person fails?

Comprehension Strategy: Making Inferences

> Writers do not always directly state certain information. Readers need to make an inference. An inference is a good guess, usually based on some information in the text and what the reader knows about the topic. Making inferences can help you to better understand a text.

A. Read the statements. Then skim the text to see if each statement is directly stated (S) or an inference (I).

......**1.** The writer's daughter is now an adult.

......**2.** Failure is an excellent way to learn something new.

......**3.** The writer takes risks.

B. Read the whole text and answer the questions that follow.

🎧 *CD 2 Track 5*

Learning Through Failure

1 Many years ago, when my daughter started school, I said to her, "I know you'll do well." Over the years as she grew up, I wished her success many times. But often, in my heart, I hoped that she would be a washout—that she would not succeed. In other words, I wanted her to fail.

2 I love my daughter; that's why I wanted her to fail. I believe in failure. Failure is the best way to learn. When we do something well, when we succeed, we do not learn anything. Rather, we just confirm what we already know. Success means doing something that we can already do. There is very little learning from success.

3 When we fail, we have an opportunity to learn. But, we have to study our failures. We have to figure out why we did not succeed. And, that is where the learning comes in.

4 We should not set out to fail, of course. We should try to do well, to succeed. Sometimes we do moderately well, and sometimes we do very well. If we continue to do the same things in the same way, we will never fail. But, we will never learn anything new.

5   Failure comes when we take a risk, or when we do something different. When I lived in Africa, I heard a wise saying: "A good cook has broken many pots." At the time, I didn't understand it. But, later I realized that it meant that a person needs to try different ways of doing things and to try new things. Life is tedious if we only do what we know how to do well.

6   I didn't learn the importance of failure until I had been a university professor for five years. In my teaching and research, I wanted to succeed. I wanted to do the best I possibly could. If I even thought of failure, I thought that it was something to be avoided. I was afraid that if I failed, my colleagues would look down on me. I was worried that if I failed, I would be regarded as a failure.

7   One day I had a terrible class. It was a large undergraduate class. Until that day, I always lectured for the entire time. The 45 students would sit quietly and take notes. But this time, I tried something different. I lectured for about 15 minutes, and then put the students in groups of four or five. I told them to discuss what I had said in my lecture.

8   A colleague of mine had told me about this. He said that his students really enjoyed working in groups. So I decided to try it. However, my students just sat there. Nobody was talking. I left the front of the classroom and walked from group to group, pausing by each circle of students and asking if they understood or if they had any questions. There was no response. They just sat silently, staring at the floor.

9   That lesson was a failure. I really felt badly. But, then I started to think about why it had not gone well. I realized that I needed to give my students clear-cut instructions about working in groups. Working in groups was new for them and for me. I tried again, a week later. This time the lesson was not a failure, but it was not a success. I needed to change some more things. Eventually, both my students and I learned how to do group work.

10   This is why I had wanted my daughter to fail. And, of course, she did fail, and I did my best to console her. I tried to help her understand why she had failed, and I encouraged her by telling her that she could do better the next time. But, I didn't tell her that failure was a good thing. This was something she had to learn on her own.

Checking Comprehension

Complete the sentences.

1. The author's general attitude to failure is that ....
   - a. failure is necessary for success.
   - b. failure leads to failure.
   - c. success can only come before failure.

2. By doing the same things in the same way, ...
   - a. we fail.
   - b. we learn new things.
   - c. we never learn anything new.

3. A good cook has many broken pots means ....
   - a. cooking can be a dangerous task.
   - b. life is tedious if we do the same things.
   - c. a person needs to try different ways of doing things.

4. When the author put his students in groups for the first time, they ....
   - a. enjoyed discussing his lecture.
   - b. asked him to join their groups.
   - c. just sat there silently.

5. The author probably thinks group work is ....
   - a. difficult and unnecessary.
   - b. a valuable classroom activity.
   - c. almost always a failure.

6. After his daughter failed, the author didn't ....
   - a. help her understand why.
   - b. tell her that failure is good.
   - c. encourage her.

Looking at Vocabulary in Context

A. Find the words in bold in the article. Circle the correct definition.

1. If something is a **washout** (par. 1), it is a *success / failure*.

2. When you **confirm** (par. 2) something, you *prove / question* it.

3. A **moderately** (par. 4) powerful politician is *somewhat / very* powerful.

4. A **tedious** (par. 5) job is *boring / interesting*.

5. When a professor gives **clear-cut** (par. 9) instructions, the instructions are generally *easily understood / very confusing*.

6. To **console** (par. 10) someone is to *comfort / upset* that person.

B. Fill in the blanks with the words in bold from A. Be sure to use the correct forms.

1. After Kimie failed the history exam, her friends .... her.

2. The test was .... difficult—not too hard, but not too easy.

3. I hate shopping because waiting in the checkout line is so ....

4. I don't like people who speak mysteriously. I prefer .... communication.

5. The police tried to find the criminal, but they couldn't .... his location.

6. The concert was a ....—hardly anyone showed up.

What's Your Opinion?

A. Answer the questions.

1. Do you think that it is important to succeed all of the time?

2. Do you think that we can learn from our mistakes?

3. Should professors give their students opportunities to take risks?

4. Do you take risks? Why or why not?

5. What has been a failure in your life? Did you learn from it?

B. Discuss your answers in small groups.

Before Reading

Discuss the questions.

1. Do you have a good or a bad memory?
2. What things can affect our memories?

Fluency Strategy: Recognizing Signal Words

Signal words show how the text is organized. Words like *whereas* and *while* can introduce conditions and exceptions. *Because of*, *due to*, and *thanks to* introduce causes; *resulted in* and *brought about* introduce results.

A. Scan the text for signal words. Match them with the information they introduce.

........**1.** because of   **a.** might not realize something

........**2.** results in   **b.** high grades

........**3.** whereas   **c.** better understanding

........**4.** thanks to   **d.** the strategy of taking breaks

B. Read the whole article quickly. Record your reading time below and on the chart on page 193.

CD 2 Track 6

Start: _____
Finish: _____
Reading Time: _____

Learning and Memory

1   *University Life*, a magazine for university students, interviewed four students about memory. *University Life* selected these four students because of their high grades in their university classes. They were asked to give some tips to maximize memory power and improve study habits.

2   **Aki Yoshida, 22, English major:** I do two things to help me learn. I say what I want to memorize over and over again. I find that verbalizing what I want to remember really helps. When I say some facts or ideas, I use my own words. This results in better understanding of the information. I think that repeating this helps it stay in my brain!

3   I like to do this with a classmate. First, I talk to her. I tell her the same information in different ways over and over. Then she does the same with me. There is another advantage of working with someone else. My classmate can tell me if I don't understand something very well, or if I am missing something, whereas I might not know it working alone.

4   **Jim Brown, 21, computer science major:** I believe studying has two steps, learning and

remembering. For me, I first have to learn something, and then I have to remember it. The first step, learning, is identifying important information, such as facts and ideas. I make sure that I understand this information.

5   The second step, remembering, is filing them into my brain. I do two things to help my memory. The first is to repeat an important fact over and over. The second is to put new information with what I already know. I think that my good grades in examinations are due to my two-step studying.

6   **Ina Kim, 20, math major:** I am a visual learner. By this I mean that I remember best when I can see what I have to learn. Just listening to a lecture or to my classmates talking doesn't work for me. If I want to memorize something, I need to be able to visualize it, to see it.

7   One way for me to do this is to write everything down. I like to do this on my computer. When I read, I always scrutinize the tables, graphs, and pictures. This helps me to remember. When I take a test, I try to remember the tables, and so on. In addition, I try to visualize my notes in my mind.

8   I try to use my visual memory by writing out vocabulary lists, theories, or math formulas. This helps me to recall the information, and it also helps me to see the way it looks on the page. When I have a visual memory, I can remember it easily during a test. Finally, when I enter my ideas on my computer or draw pictures, I can think deeply about the information. This also helps me to remember it.

9   **Yao Lee, 24, physics graduate student:** I learned a good memory strategy when I was an undergraduate. Unfortunately, I only learned this strategy when I was in my senior year! For me, the best way is to study for a short period and then take a break. For example, I will read for about 30 minutes. During this 30-minute period, I really concentrate. Then I will take a break for an hour or so, sometimes doing exercises to energize me. I do this four or five times a day. Thanks to this strategy, I'm able to memorize the material and then remember it when I have to. It really works!

10   These four students use very different ways to improve their memories to help them learn. There is no best way. Try each one, and use what works best for you.

Checking Fluency and Comprehension

A. Answer the questions. Do not look back at the text.

1. What is a visual learner?
   a. Someone who learns best by seeing something.
   b. Someone who learns best by thinking deeply.

2. What does Aki Yoshida like to do with a classmate?
   a. Talk to her and listen to her.
   b. Read and write and compare answers.

3. What two steps does Jim Brown use to help him remember?
   a. Learning and remembering.
   b. Reading and writing.

4. Writing out vocabulary lists or math formulas is part of what type of learning?
   a. Verbalizing.
   b. Visualizing.

5. What is Yao Lee's strategy?
   a. Saying something over and over.
   b. Studying for a short period and taking a break.

B. Check your answers with a partner. Record your score on page 193.

Expanding Vocabulary

A. The suffix -*ize* can turn nouns and adjectives into verbs. Scan the text for words ending in -*ize* and use them to complete the definitions.

1. .... means to supply power.
2. .... means to get the most out of something.
3. .... means to store in the brain.
4. .... means to check out in detail.
5. .... means to say something aloud.
6. .... means to picture something in the mind.

B. Fill in the blanks with the words from A. Be sure to use the correct form of the word.

1. The architects .... the amount of sunlight by building the house entirely from glass.

2. Emotions can be difficult to ...., but nevertheless it is important to talk about them.

3. When I'm tired in the middle of the day, a bar of chocolate really .... me.

4. Joey had to .... the capital cities of all the countries in Europe for his test on Monday.

5. After the robbery, the bank teller could still .... the face of the thief, whom she described perfectly to the police.

6. The art critic .... the painting for about 20 minutes, but finally decided it was a fake.

What's Your Opinion?

A. Look at these study strategies and add one more to the list. Check if you are using the strategy now, you would like to use it, or you wouldn't like to use it.

Study strategies	Use now	Want to use	Don't like
1. Work with a classmate	☐	☐	☐
2. Repeat important facts over and over again	☐	☐	☐
3. Visualize as much information as possible	☐	☐	☐
4. Study for short periods and take lots of breaks	☐	☐	☐
5. _____	☐	☐	☐

B. Discuss your answers with a partner. Give reasons for your answers.

Increasing Fluency

Follow the instructions to practice increasing your reading speed.

1. Look back at your reading time for "Learning and Memory." Write the time here: ....

2. Use a watch to time yourself. Read the text again. Try to read it faster than the first time. Write your new reading time here: ....

3. Did your reading speed increase?

Extensive Reading 6

Tobermory

Introduction

This extract from an Oxford *Bookworms* reader gives you the opportunity to read more in English. The more you read, the faster and more fluent you will become. "Tobermory" is a short story from a collection of short stories called *Tooth and Claw,* by Saki. "Tobermory" is set in England. It tells the tale of a cat that can talk. The extract you will read starts as Lady Blemley and her guests are having tea. One of the guests, Mr. Cornelius Appin, is telling everyone that he can teach animals to talk.

Before Reading

A. What do you think will happen in the extract? Check (✔) your answers.

........1. Mr. Appin has taught Tobermory to talk.

........2. Mr. Appin is playing a joke.

........3. Tobermory is an intelligent cat that can speak English.

........4. Everyone is very excited and happy that Tobermory can talk.

B. Now read the extract to see what happens.

🎧 *CD 2 Track 7*

Words

"Are you telling us that you have found a way of teaching animals to talk?" Sir Wilfrid was saying. "And our dear old Tobermory is your first successful student?"

"I have studied this problem for seventeen years," said Mr. Appin, "but I didn't have any real success until eight or nine months ago. Of course, I have studied thousands of animals, but recently I have worked only with cats. A cat, of course, is a wild animal who agrees to live with you. All cats are intelligent, but naturally, some are more intelligent than others. When I met Tobermory a week ago, I realized at once that here was an extraordinarily intelligent cat, a very special cat indeed. In Tobermory, I

50

100

found the student I needed. With him I have succeeded in my plan."

Nobody laughed, and nobody actually said "Rubbish," although Clovis's lips moved silently . . .

"And have you really taught Tobermory," asked Miss Resker, "to say and understand short, easy words?"

"My dear Miss Resker," said Mr. Appin patiently, "we teach little children and very slow, stupid adults in that way. But Tobermory is a most intelligent cat. He can speak English as well as you or I can."

This time Clovis said "Rubbish!" aloud.

Sir Wilfrid was more polite, but it was clear that he did not believe Mr. Appin's story.

"Shall we bring the cat in here and hear him for ourselves?" said Lady Blemley.

Sir Wilfrid went off to look for Tobermory.

"Mr. Appin will try to be clever," said Miss Resker happily, "but if we watch him carefully, we shall see his lips move."

In a minute Sir Wilfrid returned, looking very excited.

"It's true, you know!" he said. "I found Tobermory sleeping in the smoking-room, and called out to him to come for his tea. He lifted his head and opened one eye. I said, 'Come on, Toby, don't keep us waiting!' and he said calmly, 'I'll come when I'm ready!' I couldn't believe my ears!"

The guests all started talking at once, while Mr. Appin sat silently and looked very pleased with himself indeed.

Then Tobermory entered the room and calmly walked over to the tea table. The conversation stopped. Nobody knew what to say to a talking cat. At last Lady Blemley spoke:

"Would you like some milk, Tobermory?" she asked in a high, unnatural voice.

"I don't mind if I do," answered Tobermory. Lady Blemley's hand shook with excitement and some of the milk went onto the carpet.

"Oh dear! I'm so sorry," she said.

"I don't mind. It isn't my carpet, after all," replied Tobermory.

There was another silence, then Miss Resker asked politely, "Did you find it difficult to learn English, Tobermory?"

Tobermory looked straight through her with his bright green eyes. Clearly, he did not answer questions that did not interest him.

"What do you think of the intelligence of people?" asked Mavis Pellington.

"Which people's intelligence?" asked Tobermory coldly.

"Well, my intelligence, for example," said Mavis with a little laugh.

"You make things very uncomfortable for me," said Tobermory, although he did not look at all uncomfortable. "When Lady Blemley wanted to invite you here, Sir Wilfrid was not pleased. 'Mavis Pellington is the stupidest woman I know,' he said. 'That's why I want to invite her,' Lady Blemley replied. 'I want her to buy my old car, and she's stupid enough to do that.'"

"It isn't true!" cried Lady Blemley. "Don't believe him, Mavis!"

"If it isn't true," said Mavis coldly, "why did you say this morning that your car would be just right for me?"

Major Barfield did his best to help. He tried to start a new conversation. "How are you getting on with your little black and white lady friend in the garden?" he asked Tobermory.

Everybody realized at once that this was a mistake.

Tobermory gave him an icy look. "We do not usually discuss these things in polite company," he said. "But I have watched you a little since you have been in this house. I think perhaps you would not like me to discuss *your* lady friends."

The Major's face became very red, and all the other guests began to look worried and uncomfortable. What was Tobermory going to say next?

"Would you like to go down to the kitchen now, Tobermory," asked Lady Blemley politely, "and see if the cook has got your dinner ready?"

"No, thank you," said Tobermory. "I've only just had my tea. I don't want to make myself sick."

"Cats have nine lives, you know," said Sir Wilfrid with a laugh.

"Possibly," answered Tobermory. "But only one stomach."

"Lady Blemley!" cried Mrs. Cornett, "Don't send that cat to the kitchen. He will talk about us to the cook!"

Everyone was very worried now. They remembered uncomfortably that Tobermory moved freely all over the house and gardens at all hours of the day and night. He could look into any of the bedrooms if he wanted to. What

had he seen? What had he heard? Nobody's secrets were safe now.

"Oh, why did I come here?" cried Agnes Resker, who could never stay silent for long.

"You know very well why you came here," said Tobermory immediately. "You came for the food, of course. I heard you talking to Mrs. Cornett in the garden. You said that the Blemleys were terribly boring people, but they had an excellent cook."

"You mustn't believe him!" cried Agnes. "I never said that, did I, Mrs. Cornett?"

"Later, Mrs. Cornett repeated your words to Bertie van Tahn," said Tobermory. "She said, 'That Resker woman will go anywhere for four good meals a day,' and Bertie said—"

Just then Tobermory looked out of the window and saw the doctor's big yellow cat crossing the garden. Immediately he disappeared through the open window.

Everyone started talking at once, and Mr. Appin found himself in a storm of angry questions.

"You must stop this at once," everyone said to him. "What will happen if Tobermory teaches other cats to talk? We shall never have a moment's peace!"

Extract from *Tooth and Claw,* **Bookworms Library, Oxford University Press.**

After Reading

Answer the questions.

1. At first, what do the others think about Mr. Appin's claim to have taught a cat to speak English?

2. How well does Tobermory speak English?

3. Why are Lady Blemley and her guests upset with Tobermory?

4. Why did Tobermory suddenly leave the room?

Thinking About the Story

Answer the questions.

1. Did you enjoy reading the extract? Do you want to read more about Tobermory?
2. Will the humans be able to control Tobermory?
3. How will the short story end?

Timed Repeated Reading

How many words can you read in one minute? Follow the instructions to practice increasing your reading speed.

1. Time yourself. Read the extract for one minute. When you stop, underline the last word you read and write "first" in the margin.
2. Go back to the beginning of the extract. Read again for one minute. Try to read faster this time. When you stop, underline the last word you read and write "second" in the margin.
3. Go back to the beginning of the extract. Read again for one minute. Try to read even faster this time. When you stop, underline the last word you read and write "third" in the margin.
4. Count the number of words you read each time. Record the three numbers on the Timed Repeated Reading Chart on page 193.

Unit 7

Role Models

Discuss the questions.

1. What is a role model?
2. What qualities should a role model have?

This unit is about role models. In Part 1, you will read about different people's role models. In Part 2, you will read about an American football player who has become an international role model. The unit is followed by Extensive Reading 7, which is an extract from a book called *The Prisoner of Zenda*. The main character, Rudolf Rassendyll, takes on a different role in the make-believe kingdom of Ruritania.

Part 1 Who Is Your Role Model?

Before Reading

How important are these qualities in a role model? Add one more quality and rank them 1 (most important) to 5 (least important).

...... bravery   ...... generosity   ...... intelligence   ...... strength   ...... other: ....

Comprehension Strategy: Summarizing

Summarizing is writing the main points communicated by a text in much fewer words. When we summarize we keep only the essential information and leave out any points of lesser importance.

A. Read the text. Complete the summary with information from the text.

In an insecure world, role models give us .... These remarkable people make

a .... in our lives. Lisa's is athlete and cancer survivor, ...

Kyle's is Princess Diana because she was .... Alex admires Gandhi for

his .... methods of protest. Aleena's role models are her ....

Taka found role models in ...., and Antonio admires Pelé, the world's

....

B. Read the text again and answer the questions that follow.

🎧 *CD 2 Track 8*

Who Is Your Role Model?

1   In this day and age, we have so much to worry about—for example, wars, crime, poverty, and natural disasters. It seems that on a daily basis we can turn on the television to find some new tragedy that has happened in the world. Often our future and hope for the generations to come looks very dim.

2   However, if we take the time to look around us and recognize the role models in our lives, we can feel a sense of hope. Role models are people that we see as remarkable. They have special qualities that we admire greatly, and take action that we often respect and appreciate. Such people are all around us. They may be people from the past who have made a difference, or people in the present who are still influencing our way of life.

3   In honor of the people who make a positive impact in our lives, we asked you, our readers, to write in and tell us about your role model: *Who is your role model, and why?*

4   **Lisa, 22, Canada:** I think Lance Armstrong is a great role model because of what he has overcome and achieved in his life. Despite being diagnosed with cancer, Lance didn't give up. He used all of his strength to fight hard, recover, and greatly improve his athletic abilities. The fact that he is a cancer survivor and has won the Tour de France seven times is proof that he is a true hero. Plus, he has established a non-profit organization to help others who are affected by cancer.

Lance Armstrong

5   **Kyle, 25, Australia:** I feel Princess Diana was an amazing role model. She was a truly generous person who dedicated much effort to helping those who are less fortunate. For example, she campaigned against land mines,[1] and was very active with charities for AIDS, homeless people, and children's organizations. Many people all over the world have benefited from her charity work.

6   **Alex, 18, England:** Gandhi is definitely one of history's greatest role models. He worked for India's freedom for 30 years. He will always be admired most for his dedication to change through non-violent protest, such as fasting.[2] Perhaps if more leaders followed Gandhi's approach, we would not have so much violence in the world today.

7   **Aleena, 22, Belgium:** My greatest role models have been my teachers. I admire them for choosing a career educating children, the future generations of our world. Oftentimes the work must be tiring, and they may not get paid much. However, they continue to have great patience and a sense of duty to their students. I'd like to give much thanks to all of the teachers who've contributed to my life.

8   **Taka, 30, U.S.A.:** There are many famous role models in the world. But, I feel fortunate to have great role models within my own family. My grandfather worked long, hard hours his entire life. He started picking vegetables in the fields when he was 12 and worked his way to owning his own vegetable and fruit store. His strong dedication and commitment to supporting his family have allowed me to have such a great life.

9   **Antonio, 38, Brazil:** My role model is Pelé, the world's greatest soccer player. His natural athletic ability was simply unbelievable. He was born into a very poor family, but that didn't stop him from following his dreams. During his long and successful career, he popularized the sport and served as a respected sports ambassador for Brazil. I think every child needs a true hero, and Pelé has been that hero for many young people in my country.

1 land mine a bomb that explodes when someone steps on or drives over it
2 fasting not eating any food for a period of time

Checking Comprehension

A. These sentences are false. Correct the facts.

1. When we turn on the television, we usually hear good news in the world.

   ....

2. Role models are people who we see as common and ordinary.

   ....

3. Lance Armstrong created an organization to teach children how to ride a bicycle.

   ....

4. Gandhi was a person dedicated to change through violent protest.

   ....

5. Aleena admires teachers because they get paid a lot of money.

   ....

6. Pelé popularized American football in his home country of Argentina.

   ....

B. Mark these statements as opinions (O) or facts (F).

........1. Lance Armstrong had cancer.

........2. Princess Diana was a wonderful role model.

........3. Gandhi fasted in an effort to make change in India.

........4. If more leaders followed Gandhi's approach, there would be less violence in the world.

........5. Taka's grandfather started picking vegetables at age 12.

........6. Pelé is the world's greatest soccer player.

Looking at Vocabulary in Context

A. Find the words in bold in the text. For each line, circle the word that does not belong.

1. **remarkable** (par. 2)   unusual   special   common
2. **diagnosed** (par. 4)   identified   hoped   determined
3. **established** (par. 4) bought   created   started
4. **dedicated** (par. 5)   gave   saved   offered
5. **approach** (par. 6)   way   method   request
6. **duty** (par. 7)   imagination responsibility commitment

B. Fill in the blanks with the words in bold from A. Be sure to use the correct forms.

1. The employer's unfriendly .... was not received well by her employees.

2. Wen has the .... ability to predict events before they happen.

3. The company was .... in 1980 and has been running successfully ever since.

4. A soldier's .... is to fight, and possibly die, for his or her country.

5. Fortunately, Yuka was .... with the disease early, so she was able to get treatment and fully recover.

6. Amy has .... much time and energy to educating teenagers about the dangers of smoking.

What's Your Opinion?

A. Answer the questions for yourself.

	You	Your Partner
1. Who is a famous female role model?		
2. Who is a famous male role model?		
3. Who was a role model for you?		
4. Who are you a role model for?		
5. Which famous person shouldn't be a role model?		

B. Ask a partner the same questions. Discuss your answers. Give reasons for your answers.

Part 2   A Role Model Makes a Difference

Before Reading

Do you agree or disagree with these statements?

1. Professional athletes can have a large impact on society.
2. Professional athletes get paid too much.
3. Professional athletes should try to be good role models.

Fluency Strategy: Skimming for the Main Idea

Skimming is reading key parts of a text quickly to understand the main idea. First, read the title and any subtitles. Then read the first and last paragraphs quickly. If you still do not understand the main idea, quickly read the first and last sentences in the other paragraphs. Read quickly. Ignore unknown words and details.

A. Use the strategy to skim the text. Circle the main idea.

1. Hines Ward, an American football player, is making a difference for biracial children in Korea.
2. Hines Ward achieved his dream of being recognized by the Korean president.
3. Hines Ward went back to Korea to be accepted by those who once rejected him.

B. Read the whole text quickly. Record your reading time below and on the chart on page 193.

CD 2 Track 9

Start: _____
Finish: _____
Reading Time: _____

A Role Model Makes a Difference

1   Hines Ward is proof that an American sports star can make a difference, even if the change he is making is happening half a world away.

2   Ward, the four-time National Football League (NFL) Pro Bowl receiver for the Pittsburgh Steelers, was planning a quiet trip to Korea last spring with his mother, Kim Young-hee. It would be his first trip to the homeland he had never visited.

3   Ward, the son of an African American soldier and a Korean mother, moved to the United States at the age of one and had never returned to Korea. Last fall, he and his mother began planning a trip so Ward could learn more about his heritage[1] and homeland and see where he was born.

4   "It was something that was needed throughout my life," said Ward. "I've

accomplished everything I've wanted in my life, and that was one of my last goals: to learn more about my heritage and what my mom is about. I didn't know much about the Korean side of her, and that's a part of what I am today."

5   When Ward won the Super Bowl MVP, his trip suddenly became a major news story in South Korea. NFL football is usually not a big interest there, but Ward learned he had quickly become a celebrity in his mother's nation.

6   While researching the trip, Ward was surprised and saddened to learn that those of biracial descent such as himself are treated differently in South Korea because they are not of pure Korean blood. If Ward had stayed in South Korea, for example, he couldn't have joined the military because it accepts only Koreans of "pure blood."

7   Ward then decided to use his celebrity status to appeal to South Korean president Roh Moo-hyun and other government officials to make laws so the estimated 35,000 biracial children would be more accepted.

8   While in South Korea, Ward was introduced to a biracial soccer player who, despite his skill, was often shunned by his teammates. "I did experience the dark side of my culture, being that I lived the life those kids are going through," he said. "So if you can accept me, you can surely accept those kids who live in Korea."

9   Even Ward had no idea his words could have such impact. His message was widely publicized and attracted much media attention. So, he returned about a month later to establish the Hines Ward Helping Hand Foundation to aid biracial children

not only in South Korea, but also in the United States. The foundation will work with the long-established Pearl S. Buck International organization, which helps promote opportunities for youngsters worldwide.

Hines Ward

10   In honor of his mother, who still works in a school cafeteria in Forest Park, Georgia, Ward pledged one million dollars to the cause—a large amount of money, even for a pro athlete.

11   "I didn't go over there to be the next Martin Luther King," he said. "I went over there to learn more about my heritage. As far as laws changing, they're working on it. It doesn't happen overnight, of course, but they're trying to help against the injustice against biracial kids."

12   During the Steelers' White House visit in June, Ward met with some government officials and Korean diplomats[2] to promote his cause. Ward plans to continue his efforts even after he retires from American football.

13   "Everything happens for a reason," Ward said. "Maybe it was intended for us to go back to Korea and do some good things there." It seems he already has.

14   "You came back a hero," Korean president Roh said. "Children growing up in South Korea can have big dreams by watching Hines Ward."

1 **heritage** things we inherit from our cultural past
2 **diplomats** officials who represent one country to another country

Checking Fluency and Comprehension

A. Answer the questions. Do not look back at the text.

1. Who is Hines Ward?

    a. A famous football star who is trying to make a positive change.

    b. A famous football star who is moving to South Korea.

2. Why did Ward first visit South Korea?

    a. So he could visit his mother.

    b. So he could learn more about his heritage.

3. When planning his trip, what surprising information did Ward learn?

    a. Biracial people are not fully accepted in South Korea.

    b. American football is not popular in South Korea.

4. What kind of change is Ward trying to make?

    a. To improve equality for biracial people.

    b. To improve education for biracial people.

5. In which way has Ward tried to make a change?

    a. He established an organization to support biracial children.

    b. He has written and changed several laws to help biracial children.

B. Check your answers with a partner. Record your score on page 193.

Expanding Vocabulary

A. Many words have more than one meaning. Find the words in bold in the text and circle the meaning used there.

1. **Proof** (par. 1) means *evidence / test printing.*

2. **Pro** (par. 2) means *in favor of / professional.*

3. **Descent** (par. 6) means *ancestry / downward motion.*

4. **Appeal** (par. 7) means *request sincerely / attractive quality.*

5. **Impact** (par. 9) means *crash / strong impression.*

6. **Promote** (par. 12) means *give someone a higher ranking job / support.*

B. Fill in the blanks with the words in bold from A. Be sure to use the correct forms.

1. Eva is so good at karaoke that she sounds like a real _____.

2. The singer _____ to his fans to donate money to charity.

3. Teachers can have a positive _____ on children's lives.

4. The police think the man stole the diamond, but they can't arrest him as they have no _____.

5. A new government campaign is currently _____ healthy eating.

6. Our family is of German _____ for as far back as we know.

What's Your Opinion?

Discuss the questions.

1. How much do you know about your parents' backgrounds?

2. Are biracial people treated differently from others in your country?

3. Is it OK for Hines Ward to make social change in a foreign country?

4. What other famous athletes have an impact on society?

5. If you could donate a million dollars for social change, which organization would you donate it to?

Increasing Fluency

Read the paragraph quickly; don't stop to think about the missing words. Mark the statements below true (T) or false (F).

Mia Hamm is a true XXXXX legend. She was one of the best forwards in the sport—defenders had great XXXXX keeping her from scoring goals. She was a team XXXXX of two FIFA Women's World Cup gold medal teams and is an XXXXX gold medalist. Though recently retired from professional XXXXX, her achievements have left an impact on young female XXXXX players everywhere.

_____ 1. Mia Hamm is a well-known basketball player.

_____ 2. Mia Hamm has played in the Olympics.

_____ 3. Mia Hamm has been a role model for many young female athletes.

Extensive Reading 7

The Prisoner of Zenda

Introduction

This extract from an Oxford *Bookworms* reader gives you the opportunity to read more in English. The more you read, the faster and more fluent you will become. *The Prisoner of Zenda* is an adventure story set in Ruritania, a make-believe kingdom. It tells the story of Rudolf Rassendyll and his adventures in Ruritania, where he goes for the coronation of the new king. The extract you will read starts as Rudolph is being scolded by his brother's wife for being so lazy.

Before Reading

A. What do you think you will find out in the extract? Check (✔) your answers.

...... 1. Rudolf is related to the royal family of Ruritania, the Elphbergs.

...... 2. Rudolf gets a job.

...... 3. Rudolf travels to Ruritania but never gets to meet the King.

...... 4. Rudolf meets the King and discovers he looks just like him.

B. Now read the extract to see what happens.

🎧 *CD 2 Track 10*

Words

"I wonder when you're going to do something useful, Rudolf," my brother's wife said. She looked at me angrily over the breakfast table.

"But why should I do anything, Rose?" I answered, calmly eating my egg. "I've got nearly enough money for the things I want, and my brother, Robert, is a lord—Lord Burlesdon. I'm very happy."

50

"You're twenty-nine, and you've done nothing except ..."

"Play about? It's true. We Rassendylls are a rich and famous family, and we don't need to do anything."

This made Rose angry. "Rich and famous families usually behave worse than less important families," she said.

100

When I heard this, I touched my dark red hair. I knew what she meant.

"I'm so pleased that Robert's hair is black!" she cried.

Just then my brother, Robert, came in. When he looked at Rose, he could see that there was something wrong.

"What's the matter, my dear?" he said.

"Oh, she's angry because I never do anything useful, and because I've got red hair," I said.

"Well, I know he can't do much about his hair, or his nose . . ." Rose began.

"No, the nose and the hair are in the family," my brother agreed. "And Rudolf has both of them."

In the room there were many family pictures, and one of them was of a very beautiful woman, Lady Amelia, who lived a hundred and fifty years ago. I stood up and turned to look at it.

"If you took that picture away, Robert," Rose cried, "we could forget all about it."

"Oh, but I don't want to forget about it," I replied. "I like being an Elphberg."

But perhaps I should stop for a moment and explain why Rose was angry about my nose and my hair—and why I, a Rassendyll, said I was an Elphberg. After all, the Elphbergs are the royal family of Ruritania, and have been for hundreds of years.

The story is told in a book about the Rassendyll family history:

In the year 1733 Prince Rudolf of Ruritania came to England on a visit and he stayed for several months. Like many of the Elphberg royal family, he had blue eyes, an unusually long straight nose, and a lot of dark red hair. He was also tall and very good-looking.

During his stay here, he became friendly with Lady Amelia, the beautiful wife of Lord Burlesdon. They became very good friends indeed, which, naturally, did not please Lord Burlesdon. So, one cold wet morning, the two men fought. The Prince was hurt in the fight, but got better and was hurried back to Ruritania. There he married and became King Rudolf the Third. But Lord Burlesdon fell ill, and six months later he died. Two months after that, Lady Amelia had a baby son, who became the next Lord Burlesdon and the head of the Rassendyll family. The boy grew into a man with blue eyes, a long straight nose, and dark red hair.

* * *

These things can happen in the best of families, and among the many pictures of the Rassendylls at home, you can see that five or six of them have the same blue eyes, the same nose, and the same red hair.

300

350

400

450

500

So, because my hair was red and I had the Elphberg nose, Rose worried about me. In the end, to please her, I promised to get a job in six months' time. This gave me six free months to enjoy myself first.

And an idea came to me—I would visit Ruritania. None of my family had ever been there. They preferred to forget all about the Lady Amelia. But I saw in the newspaper that, in three weeks, the new young King, Rudolf the Fifth, would have his coronation. It would be an interesting time to visit the country.

I knew my family would not like my going, so I told them I was going walking in Austria.

* * *

Rudolf travels to Ruritania by train. He stays in a small town called Zenda. One day he takes a walk through the nearby forest to see a castle. He sits down to look at the view and falls asleep. He is woken up by the sound of people coming toward him.

* * *

Suddenly I heard a voice say, "Good heavens! He looks just like the King!"

When I opened my eyes, there were two men in front of me. One of them came nearer.

"May I ask your name?" he said.

"Well, why don't you tell me your names first?" I replied.

The younger of the two men said, "This is Captain Sapt, and I am Fritz von Tarlenheim. We work for the King of Ruritania."

"And I am Rudolf Rassendyll," I answered, "a traveler from England. My brother is Lord Burlesdon."

"Of course! The hair!" Sapt cried. "You know the story, Fritz?"

Just then a voice called out from the trees behind us. "Fritz! Fritz! Where are you, man?"

"It's the King!" Fritz said, and Sapt laughed.

Then a young man jumped out from behind a tree. I gave a cry, and when he saw me, he stepped back in

750

800

850

sudden surprise. The King of Ruritania looked just like Rudolf Rassendyll, and Rudolf Rassendyll looked just like the King!

Extract from *The Prisoner of Zenda*, Bookworms Library, Oxford University Press.

Total Words: 877

After Reading

Answer the questions.

1. What excuse does Rudolph make for being lazy?

   ....

2. How does Rudolph look different from his brother?

   ....

3. Who are the Elphbergs?

   ....

4. Who does Rudolph look like?

   ....

Thinking About the Story

Answer the questions.

1. Did you enjoy reading the extract? Do you want to read more about Rudolf's adventures in Ruritania?
2. What do you think will happen to Rudolf?
3. The title of this story is *The Prisoner of Zenda*. Who do you think the prisoner will be?

Timed Repeated Reading

How many words can you read in one minute? Follow the instructions to practice increasing your reading speed.

1. Time yourself. Read the extract for one minute. When you stop, underline the last word you read and write "first" in the margin.
2. Go back to the beginning of the extract. Read again for one minute. Try to read faster this time. When you stop, underline the last word you read and write "second" in the margin.
3. Go back to the beginning of the extract. Read again for one minute. Try to read even faster this time. When you stop, underline the last word you read and write "third" in the margin.
4. Count the number of words you read each time. Record the three numbers on the Timed Repeated Reading Chart on page 193.

Unit 8

The Mind

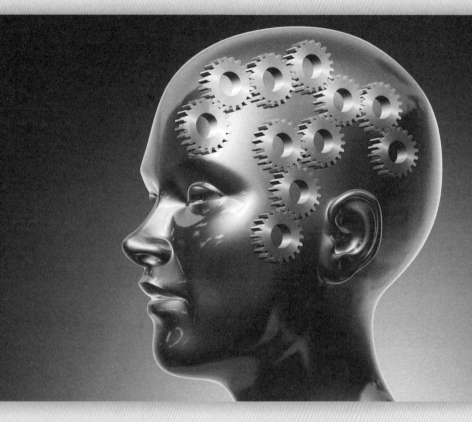

Discuss the questions.

1. What do you know about the brain and its different parts?
2. How is the mind different from the brain?

This unit is about the human mind. In Part 1, you will read about research into prescription drugs. In Part 2, you will read about the computers of the future. The unit is followed by Extensive Reading 8, which is an extract from a short story called "The Fall of the House of Usher." It is about a man who tries to help a friend "ill in body and ill in mind" who lives in a mysterious house.

Part 1   Drugs that Help the Mind

Before Reading

Discuss the questions.

1. How can we improve our minds?
2. What are some of the dangers of medicines?

Comprehension Strategy: Identifying Supporting Details

Supporting details are used to reinforce or support the main idea of a paragraph. Types of supporting details include verifiable facts, statistics, quotes from experts, opinions of individuals, perceived trends, examples, etc.

A. Scan the text for the details (1–3). Match them with the ideas they support (a–c).

........1. soldiers

........2. Connie Short

........3. people with high blood pressure

a. To show an old drug being used in a new way.

b. To show an old drug being used in a traditional way.

c. To show a situation which future drugs might treat.

B. Read the whole text and answer the questions that follow.

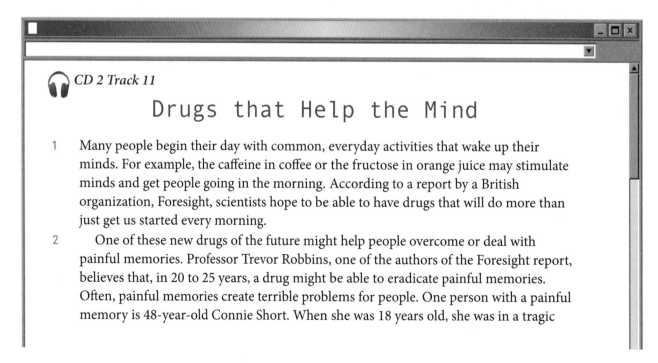

🎧 *CD 2 Track 11*

Drugs that Help the Mind

1   Many people begin their day with common, everyday activities that wake up their minds. For example, the caffeine in coffee or the fructose in orange juice may stimulate minds and get people going in the morning. According to a report by a British organization, Foresight, scientists hope to be able to have drugs that will do more than just get us started every morning.

2   One of these new drugs of the future might help people overcome or deal with painful memories. Professor Trevor Robbins, one of the authors of the Foresight report, believes that, in 20 to 25 years, a drug might be able to eradicate painful memories. Often, painful memories create terrible problems for people. One person with a painful memory is 48-year-old Connie Short. When she was 18 years old, she was in a tragic

automobile accident that killed her parents. Ever since then, she has not been able to ride in a car, taxi, or bus. This, of course, has created serious problems for Ms. Short. But, taking a drug could erase the bad memory of the automobile accident and help Ms. Short to lead a normal life.

3   Another use for drugs that could help people deal with painful memories might be in treating drug addiction. The drugs could erase memories of using drugs. This would remove the desire for that particular drug. As research in drugs to erase undesirable memories improves, it could help to reduce the harmful effects of today's illegal drugs.

4   In addition to drugs of the future, scientists are finding new uses for drugs that people already take. They have discovered that drugs that people take for physical illnesses can also help treat diseases of the mind.

5   One of these drugs is propranolol. For 25 years, this drug has been used to treat people with high blood pressure. Dr. Alain Brunet of McGill University in Montreal, Canada, has discovered that propranolol helps to reduce the painful impact of bad memories. Dr. Roger Pitman of Harvard University has also had good results working with this drug. He found that patients given propranolol shortly after a distressing event are less emotional when recalling the experience.

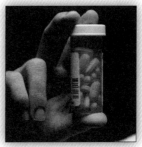

6   Another drug that scientists are also finding a new use for is modafinil. This drug was originally developed to treat a sleep disorder called narcolepsy. Narcolepsy causes people to go into a deep sleep during the day for a brief period of time. Scientists have now discovered a mind-sharpening use for this drug. They use it to reduce impulsiveness and to help people think more clearly and deeply for longer periods of time. For instance, in playing intricate games such as chess or go[1], we could plan our next move better. Of course, planning would take a bit longer, but we would probably make a better move.

7   The United States military is already using this drug. Soldiers take it to help them stay awake and alert. Some scientists think the drug could be useful for people who work through the night.

8   The effects of long-term drug use are largely unknown and may be dangerous. At the present time, we do not know much about what happens when people take new drugs for five or ten years or even longer. Often, people become hooked on drugs and cannot live their lives without them.

9   Doctors also know that the duration of the effectiveness of some drugs can vary greatly. This means that the mind drug that helps to reduce impulsiveness might cease working if a person takes it for a number of years. Other doctors are confident that these problems can be overcome. They look forward to a future where diseases of the mind no longer exist.

1 go an Asian strategy game played placing stones on a 19 by 19 grid

Checking Comprehension

A. Mark the statements true (T) or false (F). Correct the information for the ones which are false.

........1. Connie Short has terrible memories which prevent her from riding in cars, taxis, or buses.

....

........2. Drugs can stop drug addiction by creating new memories.

....

........3. Drugs designed for one purpose mustn't be used for another.

....

........4. Chess and go are games that require deep thinking.

....

........5. Modafinil might be able to help people who work through the night.

....

........6. Scientists understand the long-term effects of new drugs.

....

B. Match the words with the definitions given in the text.

........1. fructose   **a.** a drug used by soldiers to stay awake

........2. propranolol   **b.** a drug used to fight high blood pressure

........3. narcolepsy   **c.** a sugar contained in fruits

........4. caffeine   **d.** a disorder marked by falling asleep midday

........5. modafinil   **e.** a stimulant contained in coffee

Looking at Vocabulary in Context

A. Find the words in bold in the text. Match the words with the definitions.

........1. **stimulate** (par. 1)　　**a.** causing psychological pain

........2. **eradicate** (par. 2)　　**b.** acting without thinking

........3. **distressing** (par. 5)　　**c.** complicated

........4. **impulsiveness** (par. 6)　　**d.** remove

........5. **intricate** (par. 6)　　**e.** addicted to

........6. **hooked on** (par. 8)　　**f.** make more alert

B. Fill each blank with one of the words above. Be sure to use the correct form.

1. Failing the entrance examination was very .... for my younger sister.

2. The caffeine in coffee .... the brain.

3. Our landlord tried to .... all the cockroaches in our building, but they came back the next year.

4. After Aya took the drug for a year, she was .... it.

5. The brain is more complex than the most .... computer.

6. .... isn't good while shopping—stop and think before you buy silly things.

What's Your Opinion?

A. Do you agree or disagree with the statements? Check (✔) your answers.

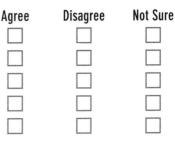

	Agree	Disagree	Not Sure
1. It's easy to get hooked on coffee.	☐	☐	☐
2. Using drugs to improve our minds is dangerous.	☐	☐	☐
3. People are already taking too many new medicines.	☐	☐	☐
4. Scientists should test drugs on animals.	☐	☐	☐
5. New drugs shouldn't be advertised on TV.	☐	☐	☐

B. Discuss your answers with a partner. Give reasons for your answers.

Before Reading

What will robots be able to do in the future? Check (✔) your choices and add one more idea.

...... make tea   ...... give massages   ...... think   ...... have emotions   ...... other: ....

Fluency Strategy: Ignoring Unknown Words

> You don't need to know the meaning of every word to understand the meaning of a text. Put your dictionary away. When you come to words you don't know, ignore them. Keep reading. Think about what you can understand—not what you can't—to increase your reading fluency.

A. Use the strategy to read the text. Mark these statements true (T), false (F), or don't know (?).

...... **1.** Today's computers will be out-of-date in 20 years.

...... **2.** Computers can control traffic.

...... **3.** When computers come back on line, we are usually distressed.

...... **4.** Future computers will understand human emotions.

B. Read the whole text quickly. Record your reading time below and in the chart on page 193.

Start: _____
Finish: _____
Reading Time: _____

🎧 *CD 2 Track 12*

Will Computers Have Minds?

1   Keiko was exhausted after a strenuous 18-hour day at her office. She was looking forward to a relaxing evening in her apartment. Keiko staggered to the front door of her apartment and looked directly at an eye scanner. Within seconds, her locked door swung open, and she was greeted by the soft voice of her computer.

2   "You look extremely tired, Keiko. Please go to the massage table and have a massage. I'll get you a cup of tea, and then I'll prepare dinner."

3   Without making a reply, Keiko dropped her briefcase, made her way slowly to the massage table, and stretched out. Immediately, a massage robot began to give her a relaxing massage. From a panel near the table, a small door opened and a tray with a cup of tea appeared.

4   Is this fact or fiction? Over the past 20 years, electronic computer technology has become increasingly complex. Moreover, it is clear that in the years ahead there will

be greater developments and advances. Just as the computers of 20 years ago look primitive to us now, so will today's computers look old-fashioned 20 years in the future.

A robot

5   For some time, computers have performed many functions, once only possible for the human mind, much faster and more efficiently than humans. These operations include complex math, such as astronomical, geological, and chemical calculations. In addition, computers control countless physical functions, such as flying airplanes, regulating traffic on highways, and digging ditches.

6   As we go about our lives, we rarely think about the extent to which computers are involved in our daily routines—perhaps until a computer breaks down. For example, there might be a long line at the checkout counter because of a computer failure. The clerk has to do everything on a small hand calculator, which takes a great deal of time and may not be accurate. When the computer is back on line, we are delighted and pleased.

7   Will we continue to be delighted and pleased as electronic computer technology continues to evolve? Keiko's computer in the short scene sketched above is able to recognize Keiko's eye patterns, unlock the door, sense her mental and physical condition, and recommend a course of action. In some sense, her computer can "think"; it seems to have a mind of its own, independent of human thought and control.

8   At the present time, computers are controlled by humans. We build computers, program them, break them, repair them, and throw them away. However, this situation will change in the near future. Extremely complex computers may no longer be under human control.

9   Will complex computers of the future have minds? Will they be able to think? Will they have emotions? Will they be able to recognize and understand the feelings of humans? At present, we cannot answer such questions, but they can lead us to think about the nature of the human mind. We might wonder if the human mind actually exists in the way that human brains or eyes or arms exist. If we believe that our minds exist, then we might wonder if our minds are tied to our bodies. Can a human mind exist outside of a human body?

10   This brings us back to Keiko's computer, the computer of the future, which is not too distant. It talks. It recognizes Keiko's physical and mental condition. It sympathizes with her as a human friend might.

11   So, one day, we humans might have to deal with this new reality. We might need to share the concept of mind with machines. If so, will we continue to be delighted and pleased with computers?

Checking Fluency and Comprehension

A. Mark these statements true (T) or false (F). Do not look back at the text.

.... 1. This article is mainly about Keiko and her computer.

.... 2. In today's world, computers are controlled by humans.

.... 3. Electronic computer technology has become increasingly complex over the past 20 years.

.... 4. Computers of the future will certainly have minds.

.... 5. Today, computers perform many functions that were once only done by humans.

B. Check your answers with a partner. Record your score on page 193.

Expanding Vocabulary

A. Synonyms are words with a similar meaning. Find the synonyms of these words in the text.

1. demanding .... (par 1)

2. walked unsteadily .... (par 1)

3. undeveloped .... (par 4)

4. controlling .... (par 5)

5. develop .... (par 7)

6. drawn .... (par 7)

B. Fill in the blanks with the synonyms from A. Be sure to use the correct forms.

1. Computers have .... from simple calculating machines to powerful tools that can assist humans in any task.

2. Many human injuries could be avoided if robots did all our .... work for us.

3. Until recently, most robots .... rather than walked gracefully.

4. Our emotions can be .... by using certain drugs.

5. The homes of our ancestors look .... today.

6. We paid 10 dollars to the man on the street who .... our pictures for us.

What's Your Opinion?

A. Complete these sentences with your ideas.

1. For me, using a computer is ....

2. Computers of the future will be able to ....

3. Computers will never be able to ....

4. If computers had minds, ...

5. Computers shouldn't replace humans because ....

B. Discuss your ideas in small groups.

Increasing Fluency

Scan the line to find the phrase on the left. Phrases may appear more than once. Can you finish in 15 seconds?

	a	b	c	d	e
1. to us now	to you now	by us now	to us now	to us now	with us now
2. our minds	our mind	our minds	our minds	in mind	your mind
3. on line	on line	off line	by line	on line	in line
4. in addition	by addition	in addition	an admission	with addition	inadmissible
5. cup of tea	glass of tea	cup of coffee	cup of milk	cup of tea	cup of tea
6. there'll	there'll	there'd	there're	there'll	there's
7. minds exist	mine exist	mine exits	minds exist	mind exists	mine exists
8. one day	one day	one way	one day	one a day	on day

Extensive Reading 8

The Fall of the House of Usher

Tales of Mystery and Imagination

EDGAR ALLAN POE

Introduction

This extract from an Oxford *Bookworms* reader gives you the opportunity to read more in English. The more you read, the faster and more fluent you will become. This extract is from a famous collection of short stories, *Tales of Mystery and Imagination*, by Edgar Allen Poe. It is the first part of "The Fall of the House of Usher." The tale is set in the house of the narrator's friend, Roderick Usher, who is "ill in body and ill in mind." The extract you will read starts as the narrator is approaching the unusual house.

Before Reading

A. What do you think will happen in the extract? Check (✔) your answers.

.......**1.** The narrator arrives at the House of Usher and is impressed with its beauty.

.......**2.** As the narrator looks at the house, he feels gloomy.

.......**3.** When the narrator enters the house, he notices many beautiful and colorful paintings on the walls.

.......**4.** When the narrator sees his old friend, he can tell that he has changed a great deal since their last meeting.

B. Now read the extract to see what happens.

🎧 *CD 2 Track 13*

Words

It was a gray fall day, and the sky was full of large black clouds. All day I had ridden through flat and uninteresting countryside, but at last, as it began to grow dark, I saw the end of my journey.

There, in front of me, stood the House of Usher. And at once—I do not know why—a strange feeling of deep gloom came down on me and covered me like a blanket. I looked up at the old house with its high stone walls and narrow windows. I looked around at the thin dry grass and the old dying trees, and an icy hand seemed to take

50

100

hold of my heart. I felt cold and sick, and could not think of one happy thought to chase away my gloom.

Why, I wondered, did the House of Usher make me feel so sad? I could find no answer.

There was a lake next to the house and I rode my horse up to the edge and stopped. Perhaps from here the house would not seem so sad, so full of gloom. I looked down into the mirror of dark, still water and saw again the

empty, eye-like windows of the house and the dying trees all around it. The feeling of gloom was stronger than ever.

It was in this house that I was going to spend the next few weeks. Its owner, Roderick Usher, had been a good friend of mine when I was a boy. I had not seen him for many years, but recently he had sent me a letter—a sad and terrible letter. He wrote that he was ill, ill in body and ill in mind; that he wanted and needed to see me. I was his only friend, the only person who could help him in his illness.

Although we had been good friends when we were young, I knew very little about him. He had never spoken much about himself, but I knew that he came from a very old family of which he was the last living man. I also knew that in the Usher family there had never been many children, and so for hundreds of years the family name together with the family home had passed straight from father to son.

As I stood by the lake, my feeling of gloom grew and grew. I knew also that underneath my gloom lay fear, and fear does strange things to the mind. I began to imagine that the gloom was not in my mind, but was something real. It was like a mysterious cloud, which seemed to come straight from the dark lake, the dying trees, and the old walls of the house—a heavy gray cloud which carried with it disease and fear

This was a dream, I told myself, and I looked more carefully at the building in front of me. It was indeed very old, and I noticed that every stone had cracks and holes in it. But, there was nothing really wrong with the building. No stones were missing. The only thing that I noticed was a very small crack which started at the top of the building and continued all the way down into the dark waters of the lake.

200

250

300

350

400

450

500

550 I went up to the front of the house. A servant took my horse, and I stepped into the large hall. Another servant led me silently upstairs. On the walls there were many strange, dark pictures which made me feel nervous. I remembered

600 these pictures from my earlier visits to the house when I was a child. But, the feelings that the pictures gave me on this visit were new to me.

On the stairs we met the family doctor. He had a strange look on his face, a look that I did not like. I hurried on,

650 and finally the servant opened a door and took me into the study.

The room was large and long with high narrow windows which let in only a little light. Shadows lay in all the corners of the room and around the dark pieces of

700 furniture. There were many books and a few guitars, but there was no life, no happiness in the room. Deep gloom filled the air.

When Usher saw me, he got up and welcomed me warmly. I thought he was just being polite, but as I looked into his face, I could see that he was pleased to see me. We sat down, but he did not speak at first, and for a few moments I watched him in surprise and fear. He had changed so much since our last meeting! He had the same pale thin face, the same eyes, large and clear, and the same thin lips and soft hair. But now his skin was too white,

750

800

Edgar Allan Poe

his eyes too large and bright, and he seemed a different man. He frightened me. His long, wild hair looked like a ghostly cloud around his head.

I noticed that my friend was very nervous and that his feelings changed very quickly. Sometimes he talked a lot, then he suddenly became silent and did not say a word for many hours. At other times he found it difficult to think, and his voice was heavy and slow, like the voice of a man who had drunk too much.

He told me why he had wanted to see me, and how he hoped to feel better now that I was with him. He had, he explained, a strange illness which had been in his family for a long time. It was a nervous illness which made him feel everything much more strongly than other people. He could only eat food that was almost tasteless. He had to choose his clothes very carefully because most of them hurt his skin.

Extract from *Tales of Mystery and Imagination*, Bookworms Library, Oxford University Press.

850

900

950

Total Words: 977

After Reading

Answer the questions.

1. Why did the narrator go to see his old friend?

   ....

2. How did the narrator feel when he looked at the House of Usher?

   ....

3. How did the narrator feel about the doctor?

   ....

4. How did Usher look?

   ....

Thinking About the Story

Answer the questions.

1. Did you enjoy reading the extract? Do you want to read more about Roderick Usher?
2. What do you think will happen to Usher?
3. The title of the short story is "The Fall of the House of Usher." What do you think this means?

Timed Repeated Reading

How many words can you read in one minute? Follow the instructions to practice increasing your reading speed.

1. Time yourself. Read the extract for one minute. When you stop, underline the last word you read and write "first" in the margin.
2. Go back to the beginning of the extract. Read again for one minute. Try to read faster this time. When you stop, underline the last word you read and write "second" in the margin.
3. Go back to the beginning of the extract. Read again for one minute. Try to read even faster this time. When you stop, underline the last word you read and write "third" in the margin.
4. Count the number of words you read each time. Record the three numbers on the Timed Repeated Reading Chart on page 193.

Unit 9

Entrepreneurs

Discuss the questions.

1. Entrepreneurs go into business for themselves. Have you ever done any business on your own?

2. Would you rather work for a company or be an entrepreneur? Why?

This unit is about entrepreneurs. In Part 1, you will read about the creators of the Internet search engine, Google. In Part 2, you will read about a female entrepreneur in Japan. The unit is followed by Extensive Reading 9, which is an extract from a book called *Chemical Secret*. It is a thriller about John Duncan, a failed entrepreneur who wants a job at a chemical factory that makes paint.

Part 1 Google It!

Before Reading

Discuss the questions.

1. What is a search engine? Which one do you use?
2. What is the most popular search engine on the Internet?

Comprehension Strategy: Recognizing the Author's Purpose

Part of understanding a text is recognizing the author's purpose or reason for writing it. These purposes include to:
- inform
- persuade
- entertain
- instruct
- advise
- argue

A. Read the text. Use the strategy to find the author's purpose. Check (✔) your answer.

........1. To persuade us to use Google when searching the Internet.

........2. To inform us about Google's past and present.

........3. To instruct us about how Google's search engine works.

........4. To advise us to seek success on the Internet.

B. Read the text again and answer the questions that follow.

🎧 CD 3 Track 2

Google It!

1   Larry Page and Sergey Brin are two successful young entrepreneurs who have affected the lives of millions of people. In fact, they have changed the way many people use computers and the Internet today. They are the creators of Google, one of the most popular Internet search engines in the world.

2   Larry and Sergey first met in 1995 when they were graduate students at Stanford University. They were not good friends immediately. However, Larry and Sergey had one important thing in common. They were both very interested in computer technology and wanted to help people use the Internet more effectively.

3   In 1996, while they were still graduate students, Larry and Sergey decided to create a way for people to search more efficiently on the Internet. They wanted to develop a search engine that would quickly find the most relevant information from the large amount of data on the Internet. With a lot of hard work and creativity, by the end of 1997, their research project had become a big success. They had created BackRub—a

unique search engine that analyzed Web links in a new way.

4   Knowing that their new search technology was something special, over the next year they continued to improve it. Larry's dormitory room became their workshop where the two students worked. Their first business office was Sergey's dormitory room. A friend encouraged them to start their own Internet search engine company. So, they borrowed money from family, friends, and professors to help them get their company, Google Inc., started. In September 1998, the young Google corporation, which consisted of Larry, Sergey, and one employee, moved into its first official company office—a friend's garage.

5   Over the next few years, Larry and Sergey again continued to work on and improve their search engine. They designed a unique, and also secret, way for their search engine to find and organize the large amount of information available online. Using this new technology, it didn't take long for Google to grow and become one of the largest, most popular Internet search tools in the world.

6   Today, millions of people all over the world are using Google. Users run over 200 million searches a day in over 100 different languages. Additionally, there are now Google offices in many different countries, including Japan, France, and Italy. The company's main headquarters has moved from the friend's garage to a large building in California, appropriately named the Googleplex. The number of employees, which the company calls *googlers*, has grown from the original three to over 7,000 around the world in 2006.

Sergey Brin and Larry Page

7   Despite great success and growth, Larry and Sergey still think it is important to keep a "small company feel." They believe the work environment should be comfortable, and that happy employees, or googlers, are the key to success. For example, the Googleplex has a cafe where googlers can enjoy free, healthy lunches five days a week. Furthermore, googlers can use the workout room, the massage room, and play video games when they need a break from work. It's also common to see googlers having fun at the company's table tennis and pool tables or enjoying a game of roller hockey in the parking lot.

8   Why did Larry and Sergey choose the name *Google*? Their company name was inspired by the word *googol*—a mathematical term which means the numeral 1 followed by 100 zeros. The company likes this term because it reflects their mission, which is "to organize the world's information and make it universally accessible and useful."

Checking Comprehension

Answer the questions.

1. What is this passage mainly about?

   a. The popularity of the search engine, Google.

   b. How Larry and Sergey created Google.

   c. Larry and Sergey's close friendship.

2. Where did Larry and Sergey first meet?

   a. In graduate school.

   b. In college.

   c. In high school.

3. What was the first thing Larry and Sergey developed together?

   a. Google.

   b. The Googleplex.

   c. A unique search engine called BackRub.

4. Which one of these is NOT a place where Larry and Sergey worked?

   a. A dormitory room.

   b. A friend's garage.

   c. Larry's parents' house.

5. According to the article, why did Google become one of the most popular search engines?

   a. It uses new technology to search through a lot of information.

   b. It is easy for people in different countries to use.

   c. Most people know about it.

6. What is Google's mission?

   a. To create happy employees.

   b. To make a lot of money.

   c. To make information on the Internet easy to use.

Looking at Vocabulary in Context

A. **Find the words in bold in the text. Circle the word or phrase that has the closest meaning.**

1. **Relevant** (par. 3) means *huge amount / meaningfully related.*

2. **Analyzed** (par. 3) means *studied / deleted.*

3. **Consisted of** (par. 4) means *was made up of / was contained in.*

4. **Appropriately** (par. 6) means *strangely / correctly.*

5. **Mission** (par. 8) means *tradition / goal or purpose.*

6. **Universally** (par. 8) means *by one person / all over the world.*

B. **Fill in the blanks with the words in bold from A. Be sure to use the correct forms.**

1. The excellent movie was _____ loved by the critics—not a single negative voice was heard.

2. This dessert mainly _____ sugar, apples, and cream.

3. NASA's _____ is to advance human exploration, use, and development of space.

4. For the final project, students must research a topic _____ to the course and write a five-page paper.

5. After carefully _____ the data, the scientists presented their results at an international conference.

6. The police did not _____ follow procedures, so the suspect was free to leave.

What's Your Opinion?

Discuss the questions.

1. What kind of personal characteristics do you think are important to become a successful entrepreneur?

2. What are the advantages of being an entrepreneur?

3. What are the disadvantages of being an entrepreneur?

4. If you were to become an entrepreneur, what kind of company would you start? Why?

5. What would you need to start life as an entrepreneur?

Part 2   A Woman with a Cybervision

Before Reading

Discuss the questions.

1. What are some jobs that usually only men have in your country?
2. What are some jobs that usually only women have in your country?

Fluency Strategy: Scanning

Scanning is searching a text very quickly to find information you want. Don't read every word. Move your eyes across the text until you find what you're looking for. Scanning saves time by allowing you to jump directly to the information you want.

A. Scan the text for the numbers. Match them with the information.

........**1.** 1987		**a.** the percentage of time Kaori spends on eWoman
........**2.** 90		**b.** the number of countries Kaori has visited
........**3.** 2002		**c.** women could be divided into groups
........**4.** 10 years ago		**e.** when Kaori co-founded eWoman
........**5.** over 20		**f.** the year Kaori created UNICUL

B. Read the whole text quickly. Record your reading time below and on the chart on page 193.

Start: _____
Finish: _____
Reading Time: _____

🎧 *CD 3 Track 3*

A Woman with a Cybervision

1   So far in her life, Kaori Sasaki has had guns pointed in her face, been shot in the leg, dodged land mines, and been to refugee camps.

2   These were some of the experiences from her job as a TV news reporter that helped shape her life to now, as the president of eWoman Inc. and UNICUL International Inc., and chairwoman of the Network for Aspiring Professional Women.

3   And those are only a few of Sasaki's titles. She's also a wife, a mother (she has a daughter and a son), an author, a lecturer, and a newspaper and magazine columnist. She was chosen as one of the 13 most successful women in Japan to lunch with then United States first lady Hillary Clinton in 1996. Yet, Sasaki rejects any suggestion she is a superwoman. She sees herself as someone following through on a vision.

4   She spends 90 percent of her time these days on eWoman, Japan's first website aimed at working women, which she co-founded in 2002. It's a community on the Internet where working women can share their experiences and learn from each other.

5   Sasaki believes in change through challenge. As a reporter for TV Asahi, she traveled to more than 20 countries—mostly dangerous places. She got shot in the leg while covering demonstrations in South Africa and had guns pointed in her face by terrorists in the Philippines. In 1987, she founded UNICUL, an interpreting, communications, and consulting company.

6   Later, when she was pregnant, Sasaki worried what clients would think. She had no role models and didn't know who to tell or when. So, she hid her pregnancy by wearing maternity suits which she bought in the United States. In Japan, maternity clothes at the time were pink frills with rabbits and bears. She worked right up until four hours before giving birth.

7   The editor of *Japan Today* dropped in for a chat with Sasaki at the offices of eWoman.

Kaori Sasaki

8   ***Why did you establish eWoman?*** When I started eWoman, I wanted to have someplace on the Internet relevant to the lives of working women and men. A place where they could share their experiences and opinions and learn from each other.

9   ***Did you have any role models?*** None. A lot of my female friends graduated from prestigious Japanese universities. They worked for four or five years and then quit to get married and have children.

10   ***Are things any easier today for working mothers?*** There are some excellent daycare centers. The problem is the number of high-quality government-supported centers is low. Most workers commute by train, and they cannot really bring their kids to company daycare centers. For things to change, men have to realize the value and importance of working mothers and having services for them.

11   ***Does your husband help with child-rearing?*** A little. He is a TV journalist, so I can't count on him for a regular routine.

12   ***Have women made progress in Japanese society?*** About 10 years ago, you could divide women into certain groups. Now you can't. When I started eWoman, the Japanese economy had been built by the elite men living in Tokyo. But now the economy is stuck because the economic world in Tokyo persists as a man's world.

13   ***How do you balance being a mother with work?*** Whatever promise I make first, I keep. So, if I promise my kids I am going to their school on Saturday, then I don't agree to do anything else.

14   ***How do you relax when you are not working?*** I like to go snorkeling and be with my kids.

Checking Fluency and Comprehension

A. Mark these statements true (T) or false (F). Do not look back at the text.

.... **1.** Kaori Sasaki created a website to support working women.

.... **2.** When pregnant, Sasaki worried about what her clients would think.

.... **3.** Sasaki is successful because she had many female role models.

.... **4.** Sasaki believes it's easy for women to balance a career and children these days.

.... **5.** Sasaki's husband mainly takes care of their children.

B. Check your answers with a partner. Record your score on page 193.

Expanding Vocabulary

A. Synonyms are words with a similar meaning. For each line, circle the synonym of the word in bold.

1. **dodged** (par. 1)	avoided	asked	invited
2. **rejects** (par. 3)	accepts	refuses	reports
3. **vision** (par. 3)	concept	desire	confusion
4. **demonstrations** (par. 5)	agreements	protests	wars
5. **prestigious** (par. 9)	unimportant	interesting	prominent
6. **persists** (par. 12)	returns	poses	continues

B. Fill in the blanks with the words in bold from A. Be sure to use the correct forms.

1. The students plan to hold a _____ tomorrow over the increase in college fees.

2. Although Michael has a lot of work to do, he _____ in watching TV too much.

3. Martin Luther King, Jr. had a _____ of a world with equality.

4. The president _____ several difficult questions that she didn't wish to answer during the interview.

5. The Nobel Peace Prize is known around the world as a very _____ award.

6. Yoshi's application was _____, so he had to start applying for other jobs.

What's Your Opinion?

A. Answer the questions for yourself.

	You	Your Partner
1. What job do you plan to have in the future?		
2. Is it easy for both parents to work and take care of children?		
3. When do you plan to get married?		
4. How many children do you plan to have?		
5. Is it more important to you to have a family or a career?		

B. Ask a partner the same questions. Discuss your answers. Give reasons for your answers.

Increasing Fluency

Follow the instructions to practice increasing your reading speed.

1. Look back at your reading time for "A Woman with a Cybervision." Write the time here: _____

2. Use a watch to time yourself. Read the text again. Try to read it faster than the first time. Write your new reading time here: _____

3. Did your reading speed increase?

Chemical Secret

Introduction

This extract from an Oxford *Bookworms* reader gives you the opportunity to read more in English. The more you read, the faster and more fluent you will become. *Chemical Secret* is a thriller about John Duncan, an honest man who needs money. He is a single parent with two children to take care of. He wants a job at a chemical factory that makes paint. The extract you will read starts as Mr. Duncan goes for an interview for the job with David Wilson, the head of the factory.

Before Reading

A. What do you think will happen in the extract? Check (✔) your answers.

......1. Mr. Wilson offers Mr. Duncan the job.

......2. Mr. Duncan accepts the job.

......3. Mr. Duncan gets along well with Mr. Wilson.

......4. Mr. Duncan is told that he isn't qualified for the job.

B. Now read the extract to see what happens.

🎧 *CD 3 Track 4*

Words

"Mr. Duncan? Come in please. Mr. Wilson will see you now."

"Thank you." John Duncan stood up and walked nervously toward the door. He was a tall, thin man, about forty-five years old, in an old gray suit. It was his best suit, but it was ten years old now. He had gray hair and glasses. His face looked sad and tired.

50

Inside the room, a man stood up to welcome him. "Mr. Duncan? Pleased to meet you. My name's David Wilson. This is one of our chemists, Mary Carter."

John Duncan shook hands with both of them, and sat down. It was a big office, with a thick carpet on the floor and beautiful pictures on the walls. David Wilson was a

100

young man in an expensive black suit. He had a big gold ring on one finger. He smiled at John.

"I asked Miss Carter to come because she's one of our best chemists. She discovered our wonderful new paint, in fact. When . . . I mean, if you come to work here, you will work with her."

"Oh, I see." John looked at Mary. She was older than Wilson—about thirty-five, perhaps—with short, brown hair and a pretty, friendly face. She was wearing a white coat with a lot of pens in the top pocket. She smiled at him kindly, but John felt miserable.

I'll never get this job, he thought. I'm too old! Employers want younger people these days.

David Wilson was looking at some papers. "Now, Mr. Duncan," he said, "I see that you are a very good biologist. You worked at a university . . . and then for two very famous companies. But . . . you stopped working as a biologist nine years ago. Why was that?"

"I've always had two interests in my life," John said, "biology and boats. My wife was a famous sailor . . . Rachel Horsley . . . Perhaps you remember her. She sailed around the world alone in a small boat."

"Yes," said David Wilson, "I remember her."

"So we started a business," said John. "We made small boats together, and sold them."

"And did the business go well?" asked Wilson.

"Very well at first. Then we wanted to build bigger, better boats. We borrowed too much money. And then my wife . . ." John stopped speaking.

"Yes, the Sevens Race. I remember now," said David Wilson. Both men were silent for a moment. Wilson remembered the newspaper reports of the storm and the lives lost at sea. He looked at the man who sat sadly in front of him.

150

200

250

300

350

400

"So, after my wife died," continued John, "I closed the business. That was five years ago."

"I see," said David Wilson. "It's a hard world, the world of business." He looked at John's old gray suit. "So now you want a job as a biologist. Well, this is a chemical company, Mr. Duncan. We make paint. But we need a biologist to make sure that everything in this factory is safe. We want someone to tell the government that it's safe to work here, and that it's safe to have a paint factory near the town. That's important to us."

"And if something's not safe, then of course we'll change it," Mary Carter said. David Wilson looked at her, but he didn't say anything.

"Yes, I see," John began nervously. "Well, I think I could do that. I mean, when I worked for Harper Chemicals in London I . . ." He talked for two or three minutes about his work. David Wilson listened, but he didn't say anything. Then he smiled. It was a cold, hard smile, and it made

John feel uncomfortable. He remembered his old suit and gray hair, and he wished he hadn't come.

"You really need this job, don't you, Mr. Duncan?" David Wilson said. "You need it a lot."

"Yes, I do," he said quietly. But he thought: I hate you, Wilson. You're enjoying this. You like making people feel small. I hate people like you.

Wilson's smile grew bigger. He stood up and held out his hand. "OK," he said. "When can you start?"

"What?" John was very surprised. "What did you say?"

"I said, 'When can you start?,' Mr. Duncan. We need you in our factory as soon as possible. Will Monday be OK?"

"You mean I've got the job?"

"Of course. Congratulations!" Wilson shook John's hand. "My secretary will tell you about your pay. You'll have your own office, and a company car, of course. I'd like you to start work with Mary on Monday. Is that OK?"

"I . . . Yes, yes, of course. That's fine. Thank you, thank you very much."

Extract from *Chemical Secret*, Bookworms Library, Oxford University Press.

After Reading

Answer the questions.

1. What is Mr. Duncan's new job?

2. How did his wife die?

3. Why is Mr. Duncan poor?

4. Why did Mr. Duncan hate Mr. Wilson?

Thinking About the Story

Answer the questions.

1. Did you enjoy reading the extract? Do you want to read more about John Duncan and his work at the chemical factory?
2. Do you think Mr. Duncan is a good man?
3. What do you think will happen in the story?

Timed Repeated Reading

How many words can you read in one minute? Follow the instructions to practice increasing your reading speed.

1. Time yourself. Read the extract for one minute. When you stop, underline the last word you read and write "first" in the margin.
2. Go back to the beginning of the extract. Read again for one minute. Try to read faster this time. When you stop, underline the last word you read and write "second" in the margin.
3. Go back to the beginning of the extract. Read again for one minute. Try to read even faster this time. When you stop, underline the last word you read and write "third" in the margin.
4. Count the number of words you read each time. Record the three numbers on the Timed Repeated Reading Chart on page 193.

Technology

Discuss the questions.

1. How important is technology in your life?
2. What are some bad points about advancing technology?

This unit is about ways that technology has affected our lifestyles. In Part 1, you will read about young people choosing to not rely on the Internet too much. In Part 2, you will read about different people's opinions of cell phones. The unit is followed by Extensive Reading 10, which is an extract from a famous book called *Frankenstein*. It is the classic story of Victor Frankenstein, a scientist who uses technology to create life.

Before Reading

How much time do you spend on these activities? Write the number of hours per week.

text messaging: ....   reading and writing email: ....

on the phone: ....   on the Internet: ....

Comprehension Strategy: Distinguishing Fact from Opinion

It is important to know the difference between *facts* and *opinions*. You can check a fact to see if it is true or false. Opinions are feelings or beliefs; they cannot be checked. Words such as *feel, think, believe,* and *should* often indicate opinions.

A. Read the text. Mark these statements as fact (F) or opinion (O).

........**1.** True friends cannot be made on the Internet.

........**2.** Gabe Henderson canceled his social networking accounts.

........**3.** Face-to-face communication is more important than online communication.

........**4.** Social networking online can be extremely effective.

........**5.** Steve Miller joined a social network to meet people.

B. Read the text again and answer the questions that follow.

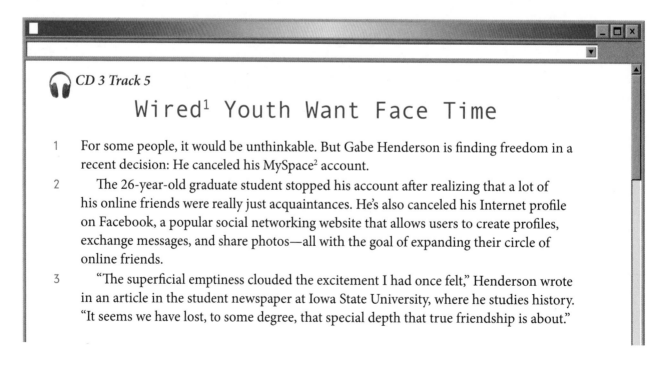

🎧 *CD 3 Track 5*

Wired[1] Youth Want Face Time

1   For some people, it would be unthinkable. But Gabe Henderson is finding freedom in a recent decision: He canceled his MySpace[2] account.

2   The 26-year-old graduate student stopped his account after realizing that a lot of his online friends were really just acquaintances. He's also canceled his Internet profile on Facebook, a popular social networking website that allows users to create profiles, exchange messages, and share photos—all with the goal of expanding their circle of online friends.

3   "The superficial emptiness clouded the excitement I had once felt," Henderson wrote in an article in the student newspaper at Iowa State University, where he studies history. "It seems we have lost, to some degree, that special depth that true friendship is about."

4   Journalism professor Michael Bugeja, who is a strong supporter of face-to-face communication, read Henderson's column and saw it as a "sign of hope." It's one of a few signs, he says, that some members of the tech generation are starting to see the value of quality face time. The excitement of their wired lives is wearing off. Also, they're getting more skilled about the way they use such tools as social networking and text and instant messaging. They are not just always using these tools because they're there.

5   Though he's not anti-technology, Bugeja often lectures students about "interpersonal intelligence"—knowing when, where, and for what purpose technology is most appropriate.

6   He points out the students he's seen walking across campus, holding hands with each other while talking on cell phones to someone else. He's also seen them in coffee shops, surrounded by people, but staring instead at a computer screen. "True friends," he says, "need to learn when to stop blogging and go across campus to help a friend."

7   These days, youth are more wired than ever—but they're also getting more worried. Increasingly, they've had to deal with online bullies, who are posting anything from embarrassing photos to online threats. And increasingly, young people also are realizing that things they post on their profiles can come back to hurt them when applying for school or jobs.

8   Steve Miller, a sophomore[3] at Rollins College in Florida, says social networking can be an "extremely effective" way to publicize events to large groups. It can even help build a sense of community on campus. He joined Facebook as a way to meet people before he started school, but also quickly learned that it had limitations, too. "I discovered, after meeting many of these (online) friends, that a good Internet profile could make even the most boring person seem somewhat interesting," says Miller.

9   He's also not always happy with text messaging on cell phones—which can be a quick way to say "have a good day," or to make a plan to meet up at a noisy concert. He's had friends cancel a night out with a text message to avoid having to explain. He's also seen some people ask for dates by texting to escape the embarrassment of hearing a "no" on the phone or in person.

10   "Our generation needs to get over this fear of confrontation and rejection," he says. "The focus needs to be on quality communication, in all ways."

11   Back in Iowa, Henderson is enjoying spending more face-to-face time with his friends and less with his computer. He says his decision to quit his social-networking Internet accounts was a good one. "I'm not sacrificing friends," he says, "because if a picture, some basic information about their life, and a Web page is all my friendship has become, then there was nothing to sacrifice to begin with."

1 **wired** (informal) connected to the Internet in various ways
2 **MySpace** a social networking website
3 **sophomore** a second-year university student

Checking Comprehension

A. Mark these statements true (T) or false (F). If the statement is false, change it to make it correct.

.... 1. Gabe Henderson canceled his social networking accounts because he had too many friends.

....

.... 2. Professor Bugeja wants more young people to communicate in person instead of through technology.

....

.... 3. According to the article, personal information on the Internet can often help people to get jobs.

....

.... 4. Steve Miller thinks that boring people can often seem interesting on the Internet.

....

.... 5. People probably choose text messaging when asking someone on a date because it's easy.

....

.... 6. Gabe Henderson feels that he lost some good friends by canceling his social accounting account.

....

B. This passage mentions some advantages and disadvantages of technology. Find two or three of each in the text.

Advantages:

1. ....

2. ....

3. ....

Disadvantages:

1. ....

2. ....

3. ....

Looking at Vocabulary in Context

A. Find the words in bold in the text. Match the words with the definitions.

_____1. **acquaintances** (par. 2)   **a.** only surface level; not very deep

_____2. **superficial** (par. 3)   **b.** very good or worthwhile

_____3. **quality** (par. 4)   **c.** people you know, but not very well

_____4. **limitations** (par. 8)   **d.** giving up things you need or want

_____5. **confrontation** (par. 10)   **e.** weak points; restrictions

_____6. **sacrificing** (par. 11)   **f.** an argument or fight

B. Fill each blank with one of the words above. Be sure to use the correct form.

1. If you want to make a lot of money, you may have to work long days and _____ spending time with your family.

2. I had a _____ with one of my employees who was late for work again.

3. I prefer _____ brand-name goods instead of cheap imitations.

4. The new model of this computer has _____; for example, it has less memory space.

5. We are _____ but not close friends.

6. She was a _____ friend who only cared about herself.

What's Your Opinion?

A. Read these uses of technology, and add one more idea. Check (✔) if you think the use is OK or not OK.

	OK	Not OK
1. Text messaging instead of calling people.	☐	☐
2. Text messaging when you're eating at a restaurant with other people.	☐	☐
3. Making friends on the Internet.	☐	☐
4. Posting information about yourself on the Internet.	☐	☐
5. _____	☐	☐

B. Discuss your answers with a partner. Give reasons for your answers.

Cell Phones: For Better, Or For Worse?

Before Reading

Answer the questions.

1. Do you own a cell phone? How important is it to you?
2. What cell phone functions do you use?

Fluency Strategy: Recognizing Signal Words

Signal words show how the text is organized. Certain signal words can show cause and effect within a text. The phrases *because, due to,* and *caused by* introduce causes; *as a result, thus,* and *brought about* introduce effects.

A. Scan the text for the causes below and read those paragraphs. For each cause, write the effect.

Causes	Effects
1. drivers using cell phones (par. 4)	....
2. daughter having a cell phone (par. 5)	....
3. having cell phones in class (par. 6)	....
4. people obsessed with cell phones (par. 9)	....

B. Read the whole text quickly. Record your reading time below and on the chart on page 193.

Start: _____
Finish: _____
Reading Time: _____

🎧 *CD 3 Track 6*

Cell Phones:
For Better, Or For Worse?

1   In many ways, technology has changed the way people live today. When it comes to communication, whether for work or for play, the cell phone has had a large impact on our lives. From young to old, the number of people who own cell phones has dramatically increased over the years.

2   And let's face it—cell phones are no longer used for just talking to others. We can also take pictures, use the Internet, send text messages, and listen to music. As cell phone technology continues to advance, they will increasingly become an even larger part of our lives.

3   We interviewed six people from six different countries and asked them: *What do you think about cell phones? In what ways are they good or bad for our society?* And here's what they had to say:

4   **Eric, 25, United States:** The worst thing about cell phones is people using them while they drive. These days, more traffic accidents are caused by drivers using cell phones. When people dial a number, text message, or just hold and talk on their phones while driving, they are not paying attention to the road. They may drive dangerously and, therefore, risk hurting themselves as well as other drivers. In my opinion, I think driving while using a cell phone should be illegal everywhere.

5   **Martha, 46, England:** Cell phones have helped to improve communication with my 16-year-old daughter. Because she now has a cell phone, I can worry less when she's out with friends. Now I can call her anytime, and I feel better that she can easily call me if there's an emergency. And now, if she's going to be a little late returning home, she either calls or text messages me—this has prevented many arguments, which we used to have before she got a cell phone!

6   **John, 35, Australia:** I'm a high school teacher in Australia, and I must say that cell phones are definitely bad from a teacher's perspective. Instead of listening or doing work in class, students are often text messaging on their phones. Thus, they are often distracted and do disastrously on assignments. I'm sure cell phones can be used beneficially, but that's not the case in the classroom.

7   **Hitoshi, 20, Japan:** My cell phone helps me to pass time during my long commute to school. Every day, I must travel two hours by train

to and from my university. This time would be a waste were it not for my cell phone! I can effortlessly use the Internet, play games, or text message my friends. Thanks to my cell phone, I don't have to suffer a boring, uncomfortable ride.

8   **Nina, 32, Russia:** It's hard to say if cell phones are good or bad for society. But, I have noticed that there are cultural differences in cell phone etiquette. For example, I recently attended a business conference in another country. Many of us who were not from that country were shocked to see how people used their cell phones. During presentations, many did not turn off their phone ringers. Some people even answered their phones and continued to talk during the presentations! I'm not saying this is bad or rude—it's just an interesting cultural difference.

9   **Song, 23, China:** Cell phones are convenient, but society has become obsessed with them. As a result, people have lost common courtesy for those around them. People discourteously abuse their phones by talking loudly in public, not turning off their ringers in crowded places, and they even drive while talking. I don't think it's the cell phones that are the real problem—it's *people*. Our sense of good manners and courtesy has been lost.

Checking Fluency and Comprehension

A. **Complete the sentences. Do not look back at the text.**

1. This passage is mainly about ....
   a. different opinions people have about cell phones.
   b. how most people think cell phones are bad for society.

2. According to Eric, some traffic accidents are caused by ....
   a. cell phone ringers scaring drivers.
   b. drivers using cell phones and not paying attention.

3. Martha argues less with her daughter because her daughter ....
   a. uses her cell phone to let her know when she'll be late.
   b. only uses her cell phone in emergencies.

4. Hitoshi's cell phone is useful to him because ....
   a. he has many family members to communicate with.
   b. it gives him something to do during his commuting time.

5. Nina noticed a cultural difference in how people ....
   a. answer their phones differently.
   b. have different cell phone manners.

B. **Check your answers with a partner. Record your score on page 193.**

Expanding Vocabulary

A. **Adverbs are words that give more information about a verb or adjective. In the text, find the adverbs for the words below.**

1. dramatic .... (par. 1)
2. increasing .... (par. 2)
3. disastrous .... (par. 6)
4. beneficial .... (par. 6)
5. effortless .... (par. 7)
6. discourteous .... (par. 9)

B. Use the adverbs above to complete the sentences below.

1. Cutting down on junk food would .... affect one's health.

2. Your life will .... change after having children.

3. Hanna .... answered her phone while the teacher was speaking.

4. Paulo did not study and, as a result, did .... on the exam.

5. With fewer jobs available each year, it's becoming .... difficult for college graduates to find work.

6. The great golfer seemed to .... hit the ball a long way.

What's Your Opinion?

A. What problems do *you* see with cell phones? Try to think of five rules to help improve cell phone manners.

1. ....

2. ....

3. ....

4. ....

5. ....

B. Discuss your rules in small groups. Decide on the three most important rules.

Increasing Fluency

Read the paragraph quickly; don't stop to think about the missing words. Mark the statements below true (T) or false (F).

XXXXX are not just found in science-fiction XXXXX anymore. For example, we can now see them in XXXXX doing work, such as putting together cars. In fact, because robots are increasingly able to do the XXXXX of humans, many people are XXXXX their jobs. In addition to work, robots are being developed for both kids and XXXXX to enjoy as entertainment.

........1. Robots are usually only seen in movies.

........2. Some jobs are being replaced by robots.

........3. Adults can enjoy robots for entertainment.

Extensive Reading 10

Frankenstein

Introduction

This extract from an Oxford *Bookworms* reader gives you the opportunity to read more in English. The more you read, the faster and more fluent you will become. *Frankenstein* is the story of Victor Frankenstein, a scientist who wants to create life. It was written more than 180 years ago, but it asks the same question that today's scientists face: How will we use the wonderful discoveries of science? The extract you will read begins as Dr. Victor Frankenstein begins retelling the story of how he learned to create life.

Before Reading

A. What do you think will happen in the story? Circle your predictions.

1. What does Frankenstein do at the university?

   a. He works hard.　　**b**. He is lazy.　　**c**. He doesn't write home.

2. What is part of the secret of Frankenstein's machine?

   a. Lightning.　　**b**. Water.　　**c**. Fire.

3. How does Frankenstein feel when he creates life?

   a. Happy.　　**b**. Fearful.　　**c**. Disappointed.

B. Now read the extract to see what happens.

🎧 *CD 3 Track 7*

Words

On my first day at the university I met my teacher, Professor Waldman, who was one of the greatest scientists in the world. He gave a wonderful talk to all the students who were starting at the university. He ended his talk by saying: "Some of you will become the great scientists of tomorrow. You must study hard and discover everything that you can. That is why God made you intelligent—to help other people."

50

After the professor's talk, I thought very carefully. I remembered the storm when I was fifteen. I remembered how the lightning had destroyed the tree. I wanted to use electricity to help people, and I wanted to discover the secrets of life. I decided to work on these two things. I did not know then that my work would destroy me and the people that I loved.

I started work the next day. I worked very hard and soon Professor Waldman and I realized that I could learn to be a very good scientist.

The professor helped me very much, and other important scientists who were his friends helped me, too. I was interested in my work and I did not take one day's vacation during the next two years. I did not go home, and my letters to my family were very short.

After two years I had discovered many things and I built a scientific machine that was better than anything in the university. My machine would help me answer the most important question of all. How does life begin? Is it possible to put life into dead things? To answer these questions about life I had to learn first about death. I had to watch bodies from the moment when they died and the warm life left them. In the hospital and in the university, I watched the dying and the dead. Day after day, month after month, I followed death. It was a dark and terrible time.

Then one day, the answer came to me. Suddenly I was sure that I knew the secret of life. I knew that I could put life into a body that was not alive.

I worked harder and harder now. I slept for only a short time each night, and I did not eat much food. I wrote to my family less often. But they loved me and did not stop writing to me. They said they understood how busy I was. They did not want me to stop work to write or to see them. They would wait until I had more time. They hoped to see me very soon.

The professors realized that I was doing very important work, and so they gave me my own laboratory. There was a small apartment above the laboratory, where I lived, and sometimes I stayed inside the building for a week and did not go out.

Above the laboratory I built a very tall mast. It was 150 meters high, and higher than the tallest building in the city. The mast could catch lightning and could send the electricity down to my machine in the laboratory. I had never forgotten the lightning that had destroyed the tree. There had been so much power in the electricity of that lightning. I believed I could use that electricity to give life to things that were dead.

I will say no more than that. The secret of my machine must die with me. I was a very clever scientist, but I did not realize then what a terrible mistake I was making.

* * *

In my laboratory I made a body. I bought or stole all the pieces of human bodies that I needed, and slowly and carefully, I put them all together.

I did not let anybody enter my laboratory or my apartment while I was doing this awful work. I was afraid to tell anybody my terrible secret.

I had wanted to make a beautiful man, but the face of the creature was horrible. Its skin was thin and yellow, and its eyes were as yellow as its skin. Its long black hair and white teeth were almost beautiful, but the rest of the face was very ugly.

Its legs and arms were the right shape, but they were huge. I had to use big pieces because it was too difficult to join small pieces together. My creature was two and a half meters tall.

For a year I had worked to make this creature, but now it looked terrible and frightening. I almost decided to destroy it. But I could not. I had to know if I could put life into it.

    I joined the body to the wires from my machine. More wires joined the machine to the mast. I was sure that my machine could use electricity from lightning to give life to the body. I watched and waited. Two days later I saw dark clouds in the sky, and I knew that a storm was coming. At about one o'clock in the morning the lightning came. My mast began to do its work immediately, and the electricity from the lightning traveled down the mast to my machine. Would the machine work?

800

850

At first nothing happened. But after a few minutes I saw the creature's body begin to move. Slowly, terribly, the body came alive. Its arms and legs began to move, and slowly it sat up.

The dead body had been an ugly thing, but alive, it was much more horrible. Suddenly I wanted to escape from it. I ran out of the laboratory, and locked the door. I was filled with fear at what I had done.

Extract from *Frankenstein,* **Bookworms Library, Oxford University Press.**

900

Total Words: 933

After Reading

Answer the questions.

1. How did Victor Frankenstein's teachers feel about him?

   ....

2. What natural event taught Frankenstein about nature's power?

   ....

3. What did Frankenstein use to bring lightning down from the sky?

   ....

4. How did Frankenstein get pieces of human bodies?

   ....

Thinking About the Story

Answer the questions.

1. Did you enjoy reading the extract? Do you want to read more about Victor Frankenstein?
2. Do you think Frankenstein really created life?
3. What do you think will happen to the creature that Frankenstein created?

Timed Repeated Reading

How many words can you read in one minute? Follow the instructions to practice increasing your reading speed.

1. Time yourself. Read the extract for one minute. When you stop, underline the last word you read and write "first" in the margin.
2. Go back to the beginning of the extract. Read again for one minute. Try to read faster this time. When you stop, underline the last word you read and write "second" in the margin.
3. Go back to the beginning of the extract. Read again for one minute. Try to read even faster this time. When you stop, underline the last word you read and write "third" in the margin.
4. Count the number of words you read each time. Record the three numbers on the Timed Repeated Reading Chart on page 193.

Happiness

Discuss the questions.

1. Is there a secret to happiness in life?
2. What are the best ways to cheer up an unhappy friend?

This unit is about happiness. In Part 1, you will read about jobs that make people happy. In Part 2, you will read about the nature of laughter. The unit is followed by Extensive Reading 11, which is an extract from a book called *A Christmas Carol*. It is about the strange events that happen to an unhappy and lonely man one Christmas.

Before Reading

Discuss the questions.

1. Do you think most people are happy with their jobs?
2. Is salary the most important thing in deciding to take the job?

Comprehension Strategy: Identifying Meaning from Context

You can often guess the meaning of words you don't know from the context. Think about the topic. Look at sentences before and after the word. They may give clues such as examples, contrasts, or synonyms that help identify the unknown word.

A. Find the words in bold in the text. Use the strategy to work out the meanings, then circle the answers.

1. **Apprehensive** (par. 3) probably means *worried* / *delighted*.
2. **Amenable** (par. 7) probably means *unwilling* / *willing*.
3. **Stashed away** (par. 9) probably means *saved* / *spent*.

B. Read the text again and answer the questions that follow.

CD 3 Track 8

Job Happiness

1   Pat Mahoney loves her job. The 23-year-old university graduate is a hairstylist in London and does not want to do anything else. While a university student, Pat needed money. She saw an ad for a part-time hairstylist and applied, even though she had no experience, except having her own hair styled. The owner of the salon hired Pat and put her through a four-week training program.

2   "I loved it from the start," Pat said. "It's so much fun to meet new, trendy people, young people who want to be hip. And, they are very appreciative when I do their hair."

3   When Pat finished her university degree with a major in Asian history, she didn't even bother to look for a job. She just switched from part-time to full-time at the hair salon. At first, her parents were apprehensive because they did not think it was an appropriate

job for a university graduate. However, they changed their minds when they saw how happy their daughter was.

4   Pat's love for her job as a hairstylist is not unique. According to a survey by the City & Guilds of London Institute, hairdressers are very happy with their work. That survey interviewed 1,200 London workers about their job satisfaction. Those who reported the most satisfaction were hairdressers; 40 percent said they were very happy. Religious workers such as clergy were next, with 24 percent reporting high job satisfaction. In third place, with 23 percent claiming they were very happy, were chefs and cooks. Close behind in fourth and fifth places were beauticians and plumbers at 22 percent and 20 percent job satisfaction.

5   Four of the five jobs on the City & Guilds' Happiness Index are *blue-collar jobs*. Typically, blue-collar jobs do not require a university degree as do white-collar jobs. Blue-collar jobs involve manual labor such as moving furniture, cleaning houses, doing construction work, or driving taxis. Some blue-collar workers are not paid very well, in contrast to most white-collar workers.

6   Experts who study job satisfaction think that some blue-collar jobs, such as hairstylists and plumbers, have high happiness ratings because of the outcome of their work. People are usually very pleased when they have their hair washed, permed, cut, and styled. Similarly, homeowners whose broken sinks have flooded their kitchens are extremely joyful when a plumber comes and fixes the broken pipes. Incidentally, plumbers are the exception to the idea that blue-collar workers are low paid; they can make a great deal of money if they are clever and reliable.

7   Another reason that some blue-collar jobs bring happiness is that the workers use their hands. Hairstylists, chefs, beauticians, and plumbers all work with their hands. The City & Guilds of London Institute's report found that people are swapping desk jobs for jobs that involve working with their hands. People may be amenable to trading high paying jobs with a low happiness index for low paying jobs that may bring a high job satisfaction.

8   The same survey found that none of the top ten happiest jobs are desk workers or office jobs. The unhappiest five careers are social workers, architects, civil servants, real estate salespeople, and secretaries. Experts think that these workers have little control over what they do. They are at the mercy of their bosses. Indeed, other surveys have found that having a bad boss is one of the major causes of job dissatisfaction.

9   Pat Mahoney plans to open her own hair salon in about three years, when she has saved enough money. Pat says that she doesn't make a great deal of money, but she says that's not the most important thing in life. "We are only here on Earth once," Pat observes, "so we might as well be happy."

Checking Comprehension

A. Answer the questions.

1. Why did Pat want a part-time job?

   ....

2. Why did Pat like her job from the beginning?

   ....

3. In the survey conducted by the City & Guilds of London, who had the most job satisfaction?

   ....

4. What are blue-collar jobs?

   ....

5. Why are desk workers often unhappy with their jobs?

   ....

B. Match the jobs with the descriptions from the text.

.... 1. Architects	**a.** can make a great deal of money.
.... 2. Plumbers	**b.** require a university degree.
.... 3. Hairdressers	**c.** are third happiest on the City & Guilds survey.
.... 4. White-collar jobs	**d.** are one of the five unhappiest careers.
.... 5. Chefs	**e.** have the most job satisfaction.

Looking at Vocabulary in Context

A. Find the words in bold in the text. Circle the word or phrase that is closest in meaning.

1. **Salon** (par. 1) means *restaurant / shop*.

2. **Appreciative** (par. 2) means *beautiful / thankful*.

3. **Manual** (par. 5) means *physical / mental*.

4. **Outcome** (par. 6) means *satisfaction / result*.

5. **Swapping** (par. 7) means *exchanging / taking*.

6. **At the mercy of** (par. 8) means *dependent on / independent of*.

B. Fill in the blanks with the words in bold from A. Be sure to use the correct forms.

Lisa has just finished university, and she is working part-time at a hair

(1) .... She is (2) .... of the opportunity to earn

some money while she looks for a permanent job. But, she wants to be the first

in her family to have a white-collar job; her parents both do (3) ....

labor, but they say they'd never (4) .... their jobs for desk jobs.

Lisa isn't sure what she wants to do, but she knows she doesn't want to be

(5) .... a mean boss. Whatever the (6) .... of her job

hunt, she feels it will be a success.

What's Your Opinion?

A. What would make you happy in a job? Write five things.

1. ....

2. ....

3. ....

4. ....

5. ....

B. Discuss your lists in small groups.

Part 2   Laughter

Before Reading

Guess whether the statements are true (T) or false (F).

.... **1.** Humans laugh about 17 times a day.

.... **2.** Most humans laugh more when they are alone than when they are with others.

Fluency Strategy: Skimming for the Main Idea

Skimming is reading key parts of a text quickly to understand the main idea. First, read the title and any subtitles. Then read the first and last paragraphs quickly. If you still do not understand the main idea, then quickly read the first and last sentences in the other paragraphs. Read quickly. Ignore unknown words and details.

A. Use the strategy to skim the text. Circle the main idea.

1. Laughter is a powerful and positive thing with many surprising uses.

2. Laughter can be very useful when used appropriately.

3. If laughter were ever taken away from humans, the results would be terrible.

B. Read the whole text quickly. Record your reading time below and on the chart on page 193.

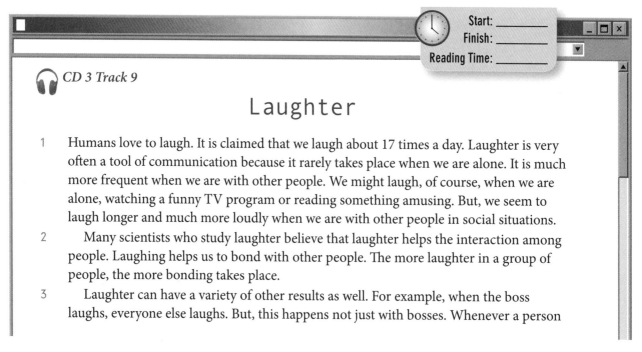

Start: _____
Finish: _____
Reading Time: _____

CD 3 Track 9

Laughter

1   Humans love to laugh. It is claimed that we laugh about 17 times a day. Laughter is very often a tool of communication because it rarely takes place when we are alone. It is much more frequent when we are with other people. We might laugh, of course, when we are alone, watching a funny TV program or reading something amusing. But, we seem to laugh longer and much more loudly when we are with other people in social situations.

2   Many scientists who study laughter believe that laughter helps the interaction among people. Laughing helps us to bond with other people. The more laughter in a group of people, the more bonding takes place.

3   Laughter can have a variety of other results as well. For example, when the boss laughs, everyone else laughs. But, this happens not just with bosses. Whenever a person

with power laughs, most everyone with lesser power also laughs. Some experts on laughter say this helps the powerful person control the situation.

4   In addition, laughter is used in some cultures to help reduce anger. If someone is angry with you, you may laugh to show that you are sorry. If the other person then laughs with you, a very tense and complicated situation may be eased somewhat.

5   In conversation, the speaker may use laughter to hold a listener's attention. Interestingly, a speaker is more likely to laugh than a listener. When a listener does laugh, it encourages the speaker to continue talking. Some research has found that women laugh most in the presence of men they find attractive.

6   Laughter is more than a tool of communication. Laughing may be one of the best ways to keep humans healthy and safe. This is what many scientists who study laughter have discovered. There is a saying that *laughter is the best medicine.*

7   Laughter might protect humans from disease. Lee Berk, a professor at Loma Linda University, California, wanted to know if laughter was healthy. He asked ten people to watch a one-hour comedy video. Before they watched the video, he took samples of their blood. He then took samples every 10 minutes during the video and three more after. Laughter, Professor Berk learned, lowered the level of stress chemicals in the blood.

8   In a second study, Professor Berk looked at two groups of people for one year after they had had heart attacks. Group A received the normal medical care given to heart attack patients; in addition, they watched 30 minutes of comedy each day. The heart attack patients in Group B received only medical care. At the end of the year, the people in Group A had lower blood pressure, lower levels of stress chemicals in their blood, and, most importantly, fewer repeat heart attacks.

9   Studies have also shown that laughter helps our bodies fight stress and disease. This means that a person who laughs a lot is less likely to become sick than a person who seldom laughs. If you are a person who doesn't laugh very much, there are some things you can do to start laughing. The first thing is to think about what makes you laugh. Observe yourself. Do you laugh a lot when you watch a certain television program? Do you enjoy going to movies? Whatever it is, try to do it as often as possible. Another thing you can do is to try to be with funny people, people who laugh a lot.

10   Scientists who study laughter also point out another benefit of laughter—it is free. It doesn't cost anything to laugh.

Checking Fluency and Comprehension

A. Answer these questions. Do not look at the passage.

1. When is laughter more frequent?
   - **a.** When we are alone.
   - **b.** When we are in social situations.

2. Why do humans laugh?
   - **a.** To get closer to other people.
   - **b.** To show appreciation.

3. For what purpose can a powerful person use laughter?
   - **a.** To make friends.
   - **b.** To control the situation.

4. Who is more likely to laugh in a conversation?
   - **a.** The speaker.
   - **b.** The listener.

5. How does laughter affect our health?
   - **a.** It may protect us from disease.
   - **b.** It doesn't have any effect.

B. Compare your answers with a partner. Record your score on page 193.

Expanding Vocabulary

A. Synonyms are words with a similar meaning. Find synonyms for these words in the text.

1. funny .... (par 1)

2. connect .... (par 2)

3. relaxed .... (par 4)

4. specimens .... (par 7)

5. humor .... (par 8)

6. indicate .... (par 10)

B. Fill in the blanks with the synonyms from A. Be sure to use the correct forms.

1. The doctor took a _____ of skin from Hye-ri's arm.

2. Jack tells great jokes; they're almost always _____.

3. His job stress was _____ when he hired an assistant.

4. A truly good friend will _____ your faults and mistakes.

5. I hate to go to sad movies; I really like _____.

6. Our class has really _____; we all feel like friends now.

What's Your Opinion?

Discuss these questions in small groups.

1. Which comedians do you think are the funniest?

2. How would you describe your own laugh?

3. Do any animals laugh?

4. When is laughing considered rude?

5. How would you describe your sense of humor?

Increasing Fluency

Scan the line to find the phrase on the left. Phrases may appear more than once. Can you finish in 15 seconds?

	a	b	c	d	e
1. love to	love to	like to	love to	to love	love two
2. what for	what for	for what	was for	what for	were for
3. in tow	in tow	into	is low	tow in	in tow
4. more of	move of	more of	more for	more than	more on
5. in the blood	in the blood	in the blood	in the belief	in his blood	in the mood
6. it is free	is it free	it is free	free it is	if it free	it is free
7. try to be	try to see	try to be	true to be	try to be	tried to be
8. doesn't cost	doesn't cut	don't cost	doesn't cost	didn't cost	doesn't coast

A Christmas Carol

Introduction

This extract from an Oxford *Bookworms* reader gives you the opportunity to read more in English. The more you read, the faster and more fluent you will become. *A Christmas Carol*, set in London, was written by the famous English writer Charles Dickens. It is the classic story of Ebenezer Scrooge. Scrooge is an angry, mean, unhappy, and lonely man. But, something happens to him on the night before Christmas one year, when he is visited by the ghost of his business partner, Jacob Marley. The extract you will read begins with a description of Scrooge and his workplace.

Before Reading

A. What do you think you will find out in the extract? Check (✔) your answers.

...... 1. Scrooge is a popular man in the city.

...... 2. Scrooge treats his employee badly.

...... 3. Scrooge thinks Christmas is a silly holiday.

...... 4. Scrooge accepts an invitation from his nephew to Christmas dinner.

B. Now read the extract to see what happens.

🎧 *CD 3 Track 10*

Words

It is important to remember that Jacob Marley was dead. Did Scrooge know that? Of course he did. Scrooge and Marley had been partners in London for many years, and excellent men of business they were, too. When Marley died, Scrooge continued with the business alone. Both names still stood above the office door: Scrooge and Marley. Sometimes people who were new to the business called Scrooge, Scrooge, and sometimes Marley, but he answered to both names. He did not care what name they called him. The only thing that mattered to him was the business, and making money.

50

100   Oh! He was a hard, clever, mean old man, Scrooge was! There was nothing warm or open about him. He lived a secretive, lonely life, and took no interest in other people at all. The cold inside him made his eyes red, his thin lips blue, and his voice high and angry. It put white frost on his old head, his eyebrows, and his chin. The frost in his heart made the air around him cold, too. In the hottest days of summer his office was as cold as ice, and it was just as cold in winter.

       Nobody ever stopped him in the street to say, with a happy smile, "My dear Scrooge, how are you? When will you come to see me?" No poor man asked him for money, no children asked him the time, no man or woman ever, in all his life, asked him the way. Animals as well as people were afraid of him. Dogs used to hide in doorways when they saw him coming. But what did Scrooge care! It was just what he wanted. He liked being on the edge of people's busy lives, while warning everyone to keep away from him.

       One Christmas Eve, old Scrooge was working busily in his office. It was cold, frosty, foggy weather. Outside it

was already dark, although it was only three o'clock in the afternoon, and there were candles in all the office windows. The fog covered everything, like a thick gray blanket.

Scrooge kept his office door open in order to check that his clerk, Bob Cratchit, was working. Bob spent his days in a dark little room, a kind of cupboard, next to his employer's office. Scrooge had a very small fire, but Bob's fire was much smaller. It was very cold in the cupboard, and Bob had to wear his long white scarf to try to keep warm.

"Merry Christmas, uncle! God bless you!" cried a happy voice. Scrooge's nephew had arrived.

"Bah!" said Scrooge angrily. "Humbug!"

"Christmas is humbug! Surely you don't mean that, uncle?" said his nephew.

"I do," said Scrooge. "Why do you call it 'merry' Christmas? You're too poor to be merry."

"Well," replied the nephew, smiling, "why are you so angry? You're too rich to be unhappy."

350

400

450

"Of course I'm angry," answered the uncle, "when I live in a world full of stupid people like you! You say 'Merry Christmas!' But what is Christmas? Just a time when you spend too much, when you find yourself a year older and not an hour richer, when you have to pay your bills. Everyone who goes around saying 'Merry Christmas' should have his tongue cut out. Yes, he should!"

"Uncle! Please don't say that!" said the nephew. "I've always thought of Christmas as a time to be helpful and kind to other people. It's the only time of the year when men and women open their hearts freely to each other. And so, uncle, although I've never made any money from

it, I think Christmas has been and will be a good time for me! And I say, God bless Christmas!"

Bob, in the cupboard, agreed loudly, without thinking. He immediately realized his mistake, and went quickly back to his work, but Scrooge had heard him.

"If I hear another sound from *you*," said Scrooge, "you'll lose your job!"

"Don't be angry with him, uncle," said the nephew. "Come and have dinner with us tomorrow."

"Dinner with you? I'll see you dead first!"

"But why won't you come? Why?"

"Because Christmas is humbug! Good afternoon!"

"I want nothing from you. I ask nothing of you. Why can't we be friends?"

"Good afternoon!" said Scrooge.

"I am sorry, with all my heart, to find you like this. I have never wanted to argue with you. But I came to see you and invite you because it's Christmas, and so I'll say, a merry Christmas, uncle!"

"Good afternoon," said Scrooge.

"And a happy new year!"

"Good afternoon!" said Scrooge.

His nephew left the room without an angry word, stopping only to wish Bob Cratchit a merry Christmas.

* * *

At last it was time to close the office. Scrooge got up slowly from his desk. Bob was waiting for this moment, and he immediately put on his hat.

"You'll want a holiday all day tomorrow, I suppose?" said Scrooge.

"If you don't mind, sir."

"I *do* mind. It's not fair. I have to pay for a day's work when you don't *do* any work."

"It's only once a year, sir," said Bob politely.

"That's no reason for robbing me every twenty-fifth of December!" said Scrooge, putting on his coat. "But I suppose you must have it. Be here early next morning."

"Yes, sir, I will, I promise," Bob said happily.

Extract from *A Christmas Carol,* Bookworms Library, Oxford University Press.

After Reading

Answer the questions.

1. Why did Scrooge's nephew come to see Scrooge?

   ....

2. Why were people and dogs afraid of Scrooge?

   ....

3. Why did Scrooge keep his office door open?

   ....

4. What did Scrooge mean when he told his nephew, "You're too poor to be merry"?

   ....

Thinking About the Story

Answer the questions.

1. Did you enjoy reading the extract? Do you want to read more about Scrooge?
2. Why do you think Scrooge is so cruel, mean, and unhappy?
3. What do you think will happen to Scrooge?

Timed Repeated Reading

How many words can you read in one minute? Follow the instructions to practice increasing your reading speed.

1. Time yourself. Read the extract for one minute. When you stop, underline the last word you read and write "first" in the margin.
2. Go back to the beginning of the extract. Read again for one minute. Try to read faster this time. When you stop, underline the last word you read and write "second" in the margin.
3. Go back to the beginning of the extract. Read again for one minute. Try to read even faster this time. When you stop, underline the last word you read and write "third" in the margin.
4. Count the number of words you read each time. Record the three numbers on the Timed Repeated Reading Chart on page 193.

Unit 12

Reading Strategies
- Comprehension: Making Inferences
- Fluency: Scanning

Culture

Discuss the questions.

1. What are some things that are unique or special about your culture?

2. What other cultures do you know about?

This unit is about culture. In Part 1, you will read a letter from a young woman who experiences some cross-cultural communication issues while living in another country. In Part 2, you will read about culture shock. The unit is followed by Extensive Reading 12, which is an extract from a book called *The Secret Garden*. It is the story of Mary Lennox, a young girl who grew up in Indian culture, who is sent to England to live with her uncle in a big, lonely, old house.

Cross-Cultural Communication

Before Reading

Discuss the questions.

1. How can living in a foreign country benefit a person?
2. What do you think is the most difficult part of living abroad?

Comprehension Strategy: Making Inferences

Writers do not always directly state certain information. Readers need to *make an inference*. An inference is a good guess, usually based on some information in the text and what the reader knows about the topic. Making inferences can help you to better understand a text.

A. **Use the strategy to read the text. What can you infer from each of the following paragraphs? Circle the correct answer.**

1. Paragraph 5: The landlord was *happy / unhappy* about Jan using the attic.
2. Paragraph 6: The landlord was *satisfied / unsatisfied* with the price Jan suggested.
3. Paragraph 7: The landlord would like Jan to *give him her things / pay more money*.

B. **Read the text again and answer the questions that follow.**

🎧 *CD 3 Track 11*

Cross-Cultural Communication

1   *People from different cultures have different ways of communicating—not just with the languages they use, but also with the communication strategies typical of their respective cultures. For example, some cultures tend to be clear and direct in their style of communication. In contrast, other cultures utilize indirect communication techniques to convey*  *their messages. These very different communication strategies can often cause confusion, misunderstanding, and sometimes hard feelings between people of different cultures.*

2   *To give an example, American Jan Smith has just finished a training program for doing volunteer work in a foreign country. She is now settled in at her site and has written a letter to her friend, Gavin, from the training program. In this letter, Jan recounts the experience she recently had negotiating her living arrangements.*

---

3   Dear Gavin,

    How are you doing? I've heard so much about your part of the country. I've decided I will have to come and see for myself, maybe early next year. Will you be around in January?

4   I have had a difficult time understanding this country, which I was more or less expecting. Some things have gone quite smoothly; others I haven't even begun to resolve yet. By far the most interesting part of settling in was trying to rent a room. I had this amazing conversation with my landlord; it was the kind of cross-cultural incident they told us about in training—the kind where you are thinking one thing is happening and the other person is thinking something entirely different.

5   Here's what happened. I found a room I liked in a nice house and met with the landlord to discuss terms and price. I wanted to use the attic to store some of my things, as my room had no extra space at all. I asked if it would be OK, and he said "Yes. If you like." Then he started telling a story, which I didn't understand clearly, about how in his culture the aim in life is to free ourselves of material possessions as we get older. These things blind us to the more important truths that we should be looking for if we're ever going to understand the meaning of life. I'm sure he's right, but I just wanted to rent a room.

6   Next, it was time to talk about price. When I asked him how much he would charge, he blushed and said he had no idea. "Why don't you suggest a price?" he asked. I know what the common rate is in this town, so I told him 200. "That's good," he said. "Don't you think?" I said I thought it was fine, and asked him whether I needed to sign a contract, and when I might be able to move in. He said it was not necessary to sign anything, and then asked me if I was sure I was happy with the price. I assured him I was.

7   He looked surprised, and then asked me if I thought the room had enough space for all my possessions. "Americans have so many nice and useful things," he said. I said that if I could store some things in his attic, as he had promised, I would be fine. "Ah, yes," he said. "My attic. My poor, little attic. And all your wonderful things. And so little money you are paying me."

8   And there we were: back where we started. It's much more fun in the retelling, I can assure you. But, it all ended well nearly an hour later when we came to terms and finally understood each other.

9   I meant to write more, but my candle is low, (the power is out again) and dawn comes early here.
    All the best, and write me back soon.
    Jan

Checking Comprehension

Answer the questions.

1. Who is Jan Smith?
   a. A person who trains volunteer workers.
   b. A volunteer worker in a foreign country.
   c. A person renting a room to a volunteer worker.

2. What is Jan's main purpose in writing the letter to Gavin?
   a. To warn him about the difficulties of cross-cultural communication.
   b. To inform him about her difficulties with cross-cultural communication.
   c. To complain about her difficulties with cross-cultural communication.

3. From the passage, what can we infer?
   a. Jan uses more indirect communication strategies.
   b. The landlord uses more indirect communication strategies.
   c. Both Jan and the landlord are equally direct with each other.

4. From the passage, what can we infer about the landlord?
   a. He would like some of Jan's things.
   b. He has a full attic.
   c. He doesn't keep many old things.

5. From the passage, where can we infer that Jan is probably living?
   a. In a populated, big city.
   b. In a different country than Gavin.
   c. In a rural area in the countryside.

6. In the end, what happened between the landlord and Jan?
   a. They came to an agreement with each other.
   b. They decided Jan should not move in.
   c. They were still unable to make a decision.

Looking at Vocabulary in Context

A. Find the words in bold in the text. Circle the word or phrase that has the closest meaning.

1. **Respective** (par. 1) means *belonging to both / belonging to each.*
2. **Resolve** (par. 4) means *solve / grow.*
3. **Incident** (par. 4) means *event / accident.*
4. **Terms** (par. 5) means *rules / problems.*
5. **Possessions** (par. 5) means *things we own / things we want to do.*
6. **Assured** (par. 6) means *confused / inspired confidence in.*

B. Fill in the blanks with the words in bold from A. Be sure to use the correct forms.

1. The .... of employment say that the job comes with full health insurance for the employee and the employee's family.
2. The pilot .... the passengers that the bad weather would not delay the flight.
3. The unfortunate .... last year ended their long friendship.
4. I have not yet .... the problem with my boss.
5. After our summer romance in Italy, we had to return to our .... countries and lives.
6. If you like to travel a lot, then it's better not to keep many ....

What's Your Opinion?

Discuss the questions.

1. Is negotiating rent a difficult thing in your country?
2. Have you ever had difficulties communicating with someone from a different culture? What happened?
3. Think about the communication strategies of your own culture. Are they more direct or indirect? Explain or give an example.
4. What culture has similar communication strategies to your own?
5. Are there any universal communication strategies? Give examples.

Part 2 | Culture Shock

Before Reading

Discuss the questions.

1. Have you ever traveled abroad? Where did you go and for how long?
2. What sorts of things would you miss if you lived abroad?

Fluency Strategy: Scanning

Scanning is searching a text very quickly to find information you want. Don't read every word. Move your eyes across the text until you find what you're looking for. Scanning saves time by allowing you to jump directly to the information you want

A. Scan the text for answers to these questions. Circle your answers.

1. How many stages of culture shock are there?
   - **a.** 3
   - **b.** 4
   - **c.** 5

2. When does culture shock generally set in?
   - **a.** the first few weeks
   - **b.** the first day
   - **c.** the first few months

3. Which one of these is a symptom of culture shock?
   - **a.** spending money
   - **b.** overeating
   - **c.** loss of identity

B. Read the whole text quickly. Record your reading time below and on the chart on page 193.

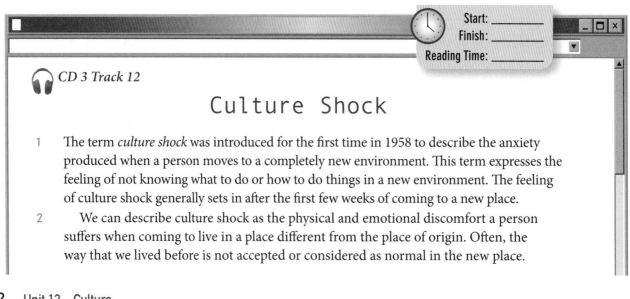

Start: _____
Finish: _____
Reading Time: _____

🎧 *CD 3 Track 12*

Culture Shock

1   The term *culture shock* was introduced for the first time in 1958 to describe the anxiety produced when a person moves to a completely new environment. This term expresses the feeling of not knowing what to do or how to do things in a new environment. The feeling of culture shock generally sets in after the first few weeks of coming to a new place.

2   We can describe culture shock as the physical and emotional discomfort a person suffers when coming to live in a place different from the place of origin. Often, the way that we lived before is not accepted or considered as normal in the new place.

Everything is different, for example, not speaking the language, not knowing how to use banking machines, not knowing how to use the telephone, and so forth.

3   The symptoms of culture shock can appear at different times. Although a person can experience real pain from culture shock, it is also an opportunity for growing and learning new perspectives. Culture shock can help people develop a better understanding of themselves and stimulate personal creativity.

4   **Symptoms of Culture Shock:**

• *Sadness and loneliness*	• *Worrying about health*
• *Aches, pains, and allergies*	• *Sleeping too much or too little*
• *Unwillingness to communicate with others*	• *Trying too hard to understand everything in the new culture*
• *Inability to solve simple problems*	• *Lack of confidence*
• *Developing obsessions, such as over-cleanliness*	• *Developing stereotypes about the new culture*
• *Missing family*	• *Loss of identity*
	• *Feeling weak and powerless*

5   Culture shock has many stages. Each stage can be ongoing, or appear only at certain times. In the first stage, the new arrival may feel very happy about all of the new experiences. This time is called the *honeymoon* stage, as everything encountered is new and exciting.

6   Afterward, the second stage presents itself. A person may encounter some difficulties in daily life. For example, communication difficulties may occur, such as not being understood. In this stage, there may be feelings of impatience, anger, and sadness. This happens when a person is trying to adapt to a new culture that is very different from the home culture. Transition between the old methods and those of the new country is a difficult process and takes time to complete.

7   The third stage is characterized by gaining some understanding of the new culture. A new feeling of pleasure and sense of humor may be experienced. A person may start to feel a psychological balance. The individual is more familiar with the environment and wants to belong. This starts an evaluation of the old ways versus those of the new.

8   In the fourth stage, the person realizes that the new culture has good and bad things to offer. This stage can be one of double integration or triple integration, depending on the number of cultures that the person has to process. This integration is characterized by a more solid feeling of belonging. The person starts to define himself or herself and establish goals for living.

9   The fifth stage is the stage that is called the *reentry shock*. This occurs when a person returns to the country of origin. One may find that things are no longer the same. For example, some of the newly acquired customs are considered improper in the old culture.

Checking Fluency and Comprehension

A. Match each of the five stages of culture shock with the correct description. Do not look back at the text.

........Stage 1   **a.** You start to feel that you belong in the new culture.

........Stage 2   **b.** You start to understand the new culture a little better and feel more balanced.

........Stage 3

........Stage 4   **c.** Your new way of life does not match your old way when you return to your home country.

........Stage 5

               d. You may have difficulties doing basic things in your daily life.

               e. Everything seems new and exciting to you.

B. Compare your answers with a partner. Record your score on page 193.

Expanding Vocabulary

A. A prefix added to the beginning of a word gives it a new meaning. Find a word with a prefix in the text for each meaning.

Meaning	Prefix + word
1. lack of comfort	.... (par. 2)
2. lack of willingness	.... (par. 4)
3. being too clean	.... (par. 4)
4. lacking patience	.... (par. 6)
5. entering again	.... (par. 9)
6. not proper	.... (par. 9)

B. Fill in the blanks with the words from A. Be sure to use the correct forms.

1. Clara's .... into Spain was not allowed because her visa had expired.

2. The student's .... to complete her assignments resulted in a very low grade in the class.

3. She sent the boy to his room because of his .... behavior.

4. Their house is always perfect. In fact, sometimes their .... worries me!

5. The dentist said I would feel some ...., but this is painful!

6. The audience's .... was clear when they started yelling for the show to start.

What's Your Opinion?

A. Imagine that you are studying and living in a foreign country. Write down five symptoms of culture shock you might be feeling.

1. I'm not able to sleep at night.

2. ....

3. ....

4. ....

5. ....

B. Discuss your symptoms with a partner. Think of some advice to help your partner cope with the symptoms.

Increasing Fluency

Follow the instructions to practice increasing your reading speed.

1. Look back at your reading time for "Culture Shock." Write the time here: ....

2. Use a watch to time yourself. Read the text again. Try to read it faster than the first time. Write your new reading time here: ....

3. Did your reading speed increase?

The Secret Garden

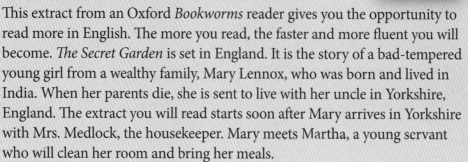

Introduction

This extract from an Oxford *Bookworms* reader gives you the opportunity to read more in English. The more you read, the faster and more fluent you will become. *The Secret Garden* is set in England. It is the story of a bad-tempered young girl from a wealthy family, Mary Lennox, who was born and lived in India. When her parents die, she is sent to live with her uncle in Yorkshire, England. The extract you will read starts soon after Mary arrives in Yorkshire with Mrs. Medlock, the housekeeper. Mary meets Martha, a young servant who will clean her room and bring her meals.

Before Reading

A. What do you think you will find out in the extract? Check (✔) your answers.

......1. Mary is very happy at her new home.

......2. Mary treats Martha like an Indian servant.

......3. Martha is a very friendly girl.

......4. Mary is lonely.

......5. Martha tells Mary about a garden that is always locked.

B. Now read the extract to see what happens.

 CD 3 Track 13

Words

> They arrived at a very large, old house. It looked dark and unfriendly from the outside. Inside, Mary looked around the big shadowy hall and felt very small and lost. They went straight upstairs. Mary was shown to a room where there was a warm fire and food on the table.
>
> "This is your room," said Mrs. Medlock. "Go to bed when you've had some dinner. And remember, you must stay in your room! Mr. Craven doesn't want you to wander all over the house!"

50

When Mary woke up the next morning, she saw a young servant girl cleaning the fireplace. The room seemed dark and rather strange with pictures of dogs and horses and ladies on the walls. It was not a child's room at all. From the window she could not see any trees or houses, only wild land, which looked like a kind of purple sea.

"Who are you?" she asked the servant coldly.

"Martha, miss," answered the girl with a smile.

"And what's that outside?" Mary continued.

"That's the moor," smiled Martha. "Do you like it?"

"No," replied Mary immediately. "I hate it."

"That's because you don't know it. You *will* like it. I love it. It's lovely in spring and summer when there are flowers. It always smells so sweet. The air's so fresh, and the birds sing so beautifully. I never want to leave the moor."

Mary was feeling very bad-tempered. "You're a strange servant," she said. "In India we don't have conversations with servants. We give orders, and they obey, and that's that."

Martha did not seem to mind Mary's bad temper.

"I know I talk too much!" she laughed.

"Are you going to be *my* servant?" asked Mary.

"Well, not really. I work for Mrs. Medlock. I'm going to clean your room and bring you your food, but you won't need a servant except for those things."

"But who's going to dress me?"

Martha stopped cleaning and stared at Mary.

"Tha' canna' dress thysen?" she asked, shocked.

"What do you mean? I don't understand your language!"

"Oh, I forgot. We all speak the Yorkshire dialect here, but of course you don't understand that. I meant to say, can't you put on your own clothes?"

"Of course not! My servant always used to dress me."

"Well! I think you should learn to dress yourself. My mother always says people should be able to take care of themselves, even if they're rich and important."

Little Miss Mary was furious with Martha. "It's different in India where I come from! You don't know anything about India, or about servants, or about anything! You . . . you . . ." She could not explain what she meant. Suddenly she felt very confused and lonely. She threw herself down on the bed and started crying wildly.

"Now, now, don't cry like that," Martha said gently. "I'm very sorry. You're right, I don't know anything about anything. Please stop crying, miss."

She sounded kind and friendly, and Mary began to feel better and soon stopped crying. Martha went on talking as she finished her cleaning, but Mary looked out of the window in a bored way, and pretended not to listen.

"I've got eleven brothers and sisters, you know, miss. There's not much money in our house, and they all eat so much food! Mother says it's the good fresh air on the moor that makes them so hungry. My brother Dickon, he's always out on the moor. He's twelve, and he's got a horse which he rides sometimes."

"Where did he get it?" asked Mary. She had always wanted an animal of her own, and so she began to feel a little interest in Dickon.

"Oh, it's a wild horse, but he's a kind boy, and animals like him, you see. Now you must have your breakfast, miss. Here it is on the table."

"I don't want it," said Mary. "I'm not hungry."

"What!" cried Martha. "My little brothers and sisters would eat all this in five minutes!"

"Why?" asked Mary coldly.

"Because they don't get enough to eat, that's why, and they're always hungry. You're very lucky to have the food, miss." Mary said nothing, but she drank some tea and ate a little bread.

700

"Now put a coat on and run outside to play," said Martha. "It'll do you good to be in the fresh air."

Mary looked out of the window at the cold gray sky. "Why should I go out on a day like this?" she asked.

750

"Well, there's nothing to play with indoors, is there?"

Mary realized Martha was right. "But who will go with me?" she said.

Martha stared at her. "Nobody. You'll have to learn to play by yourself. Dickon plays by himself on the moors for hours with the wild birds, and the sheep, and the other animals." She looked away for a moment. "Perhaps I shouldn't tell you this, but—but one of the walled gardens is locked up. Nobody's been in it for ten years. It was Mrs. Craven's garden, and when she died so suddenly, Mr. Craven locked it and buried the key—Oh, I must go, I can hear Mrs. Medlock's bell ringing for me."

Mary went downstairs and wandered through the great empty gardens. Many of the fruit and vegetable gardens had walls around them, but there were no locked doors. She saw an old man digging in one of the vegetable gardens, but he looked angry and unfriendly, so she walked on.

"How ugly it all looks in winter!" she thought. "But what a mystery the locked garden is! Why did my uncle bury the key? If he loved his wife, why did he hate her garden? Perhaps I'll never know. I don't suppose I'll like him if I ever meet him. And he won't like me, so I won't be able to ask him."

Extract from *The Secret Garden,* Bookworms Library, Oxford University Press.

After Reading

Answer the questions.

1. How did Mary feel in her new home?

   ....

2. What is the meaning of "Tha' canna' dress thysen?"

   ....

3. How is the weather?

   ....

4. What happened to the key for the secret garden?

   ....

Thinking About the Story

Answer the questions.

1. Did you enjoy reading the extract? Do you want to read more about Mary?
2. Do you think Mary will change to a nice young girl?
3. What do you think is in the secret garden?

Timed Repeated Reading

How many words can you read in one minute? Follow the instructions to practice increasing your reading speed.

1. Time yourself. Read the extract for one minute. When you stop, underline the last word you read and write "first" in the margin.
2. Go back to the beginning of the extract. Read again for one minute. Try to read faster this time. When you stop, underline the last word you read and write "second" in the margin.
3. Go back to the beginning of the extract. Read again for one minute. Try to read even faster this time. When you stop, underline the last word you read and write "third" in the margin.
4. Count the number of words you read each time. Record the three numbers on the Timed Repeated Reading Chart on page 193.

Reading Rate Chart

Time \ Unit	1	2	3	4	5	6	7	8	9	10	11	12	Rate (words per minute)
1:00													600
1:15													480
1:30													400
1:45													342
2:00													300
2:15													266
2:30													240
2:45													218
3:00													200
3:15													184
3:30													171
3:45													160
4:00													150
4:15													141
4:30													133
4:45													126
5:00													120
5:15													114
5:30													109
5:45													104
6:00													100
6:15													96
6:30													92
6:45													88
7:00													85
7:15													82
7:30													80
7:45													77
8:00													75
Question score (out of 5)													

Timed Repeated Reading Chart

Extensive Reading	1	2	3	4	5	6	7	8	9	10	11	12
1st try												
2nd try												
3rd try												

Vocabulary Index

OXFORD
UNIVERSITY PRESS

198 Madison Avenue
New York, NY 10016 USA

Great Clarendon Street, Oxford OX2 6DP UK

Oxford University Press is a department of the University of Oxford.
It furthers the University's objective of excellence in research, scholarship,
and education by publishing worldwide in

Oxford   New York

Auckland   Cape Town   Dar es Salaam   Hong Kong   Karachi
Kuala Lumpur   Madrid   Melbourne   Mexico City   Nairobi
New Delhi   Shanghai   Taipei   Toronto

With offices in

Argentina   Austria   Brazil   Chile   Czech Republic   France   Greece
Guatemala   Hungary   Italy   Japan   Poland   Portugal   Singapore
South Korea   Switzerland   Thailand   Turkey   Ukraine   Vietnam

OXFORD and OXFORD ENGLISH are registered trademarks of
Oxford University Press

© Oxford University Press 2008

Database right Oxford University Press (maker)

Editorial Director: Sally Yagan
Design Director: Robert Carangelo
Design Manager: Maj-Britt Hagsted
Project Manager: Allison Harm
Senior Designer: Michael Steinhofer
Image Editor: Robin Fadool
Manufacturing Manager: Shanta Persaud
Manufacturing Controller: Zainaltu Jawat Ali

ISBN: 978 0 19 475815 4

Printed in Hong Kong

Printing (last digit) 10   9   8   7   6   5   4   3   2   1

Acknowledgments:

We would like to thank the following for permission to reproduce photographs:
Cover photograph: Veer; Interior photographs: Fancy Photography/Veer:
p. 1; Marka/Agefoto Stock: Piersilvio Ongaro p. 3; SuperStock: Veer:
Angelo Cavalli p. 17; Punchstock: p. 19; Digital Vision Photography/
Veer: p. 23; Alamy: Reino Hanninen p. 28; Alamy: Larry Lilac p. 33;
Pictorial Press Ltd/Alamy: p. 35; Jupiter Images: p. 39; Art Achive: p. 45;
Perry Stock: John Perry p. 49; Oscar Williams: p. 55; Masterfile: p. 65;
Covered Images/ASP via Getty Images: Sean Rowland p. 71; Travelpix
Ltd/The Image Bank/Getty Images: p. 77; Age FotoStock: Pedro Coll p. 81;
Masterfile: p. 83; Images.com/Corbis: p. 87; Masterfile: Rommel p. 97;
Associated Press: Peter Dejong p. 99; Getty Images: Joe Robbins p. 103;
AA World Travel Topfoto/The Image Works: Tony Souter p. 109; K-Photos/
Alamy: p. 113; PunchStock: 115; Taxi/Getty Images: Javier Pierini p. 119;
Superstock: p. 127; Corbis: 129; Gautam Singh p. 131; International
Conference for Women in Business: 135; Age FotoStock: Bjorn Svensson
p. 141; Alamy: Rob Bartee p. 142; Masterfile: Ken Davies p. 145; WorldFoto:
Paul Souders p. 151; Solus Photography/Veer: Tomas Rodriguez p. 161;
Photo image100/Corbis/PunchStock: p. 163; Corbis/Veer: 167; Visum/The
Image Works: Dirk Gebhardt p. 177; Punch Stock/Digital Vision: 179;
Masterfile: Damir Frkovic p. 190.

Illustrations by: Nick Harris: pp. 11, 13; Jan McCafferty: pp. 27, 29; Rachel
Birkett: pp. 43, 46; Ramsay Gibb: pp. 59, 62; William Rowsell: pp. 75, 76,
and 78; Jenny Brackley: pp. 92, 94; Alan Marks: pp. 107, 110; Ian Miller:
p. 123: David Lloyd: p. 139; Ian Miller: pp. 171, 172, and 173; Jenny
Brackley: pp. 188, 189.

*Copyright material on the following pages is reproduced by permission of Oxford
University Press:* pp. 10–15 From Oxford Bookworms: The Picture of Dorian
Gray by Oscar Wilde (retold by Jill Neville) © Oxford University Press 2000;
pp. 26–31 From Oxford Bookworms: The Wind in the Willows by Kenneth
Grahame (retold by Jennifer Bassett) © Oxford University Press 2000;
pp. 42–47 From Oxford Bookworms: The Railway Children by Edith Nesbit
(retold by John Escott) © Oxford University Press 2000; pp. 58–63 From
Oxford Bookworms: Skyjack by Tim Vicary © Oxford University Press
2000; pp. 74–79 From Oxford Bookworms: Kidnapped by Robert Louis
Stevenson (retold by Clare West) © Oxford University Press 2000;
pp. 90–95 From "Tobermory" in Oxford Bookworms: Tooth and Claw by
Saki (retold by Rosemary Border) © Oxford University Press 2000;
pp. 106–111 From Oxford Bookworms: The Prisoner of Zenda by
Anthony Hope (retold by Diane Mowat) © Oxford University Press 2000;
pp. 122–127 From "The Fall of the House of Usher" in Oxford Bookworms:
Tales of Mystery and Imagination by Edgar Allan Poe (retold by Margaret
Naudi) © Oxford University Press 2000; pp. 138–143 From Oxford
Bookworms: Chemical Secret by Tim Vicary © Oxford University
Press 2000; pp. 154–159 From Oxford Bookworms: Frankenstein by
Mary Shelley (retold by Patrick Nobes) © Oxford University Press 2000;
pp. 170–175 From Oxford Bookworms: A Christmas Carol by Charles
Dickens (retold by Clare West) © Oxford University Press 2000;
pp. 186–191 From Oxford Bookworms: The Secret Garden by Frances
Hodgson Burnett (retold by Clare West) © Oxford University Press 2000

*The publishers would like to thank the following for their permission to reproduce
copyright material:* pp. 18–19, "Tourist Bound for Turkey ends up in
Tourquay," by Sean O'Neill. Reprinted and adapted with permission
from Shelley Bishton. pp. 22–23, "Coping with your travel companion,"
published in CNN.com on April 8, 2005. Reprinted and adapted with
permission from Diann Henry. pp. 38–39, "The Top Seven Signs that
Someone is Lying to You," with permission to republish from the Free
SixWise.com Personal Success Newsletter. pp. 66–67, "Boys survive week
at sea on jellyfish and rainwater," by Tom Leonard. Reprinted and adapted
with permission from Shelley Bishton. pp. 70–71, Copyright © 2005,
"From Surfer to Celebrity" by Kidzworld.com Inc. (dba Kidzworld Media),
http://www.kidzworld.com. Reprinted with permission. pp. 102–103,
"Super Bowl MVP Hines Ward Uses Fame to Push for Social Change,"
Copyright © Associated Press. Reprinted and adapted with permission
from Amy Blackburn. pp. 134–135, "Woman with a Cybervision," by
JapanToday.com. Reprinted and adapted with permission from Mark
Devlin. pp. 146–147, "Wired-weary youth seek face time," by Martha
Irvine. Reprinted and adapted with permission from Amy Blackburn.
pp. 178–179, Reprinted with permission from **Culture Matters: The
Peace Corps Cross-Cultural Workbook,** produced by the Peace Corps,
Washington, D.C., (peacecorps.gov/library). pp. 182–183, "Culture Shock,"
by Dr. Carmen Guanipa. Reprinted and adapted with permission from
John Ho.

*We would like to thank the following teachers, whose reviews, comments, and
suggestions contributed to the development of this series:*
Young-joo Bang, Myongji University, Korea; Pi-i Chuang, Chung Yuan
Christian University, Taiwan; Li-hui Chen, Tunghai University, Taiwan;
Larry Cisar, Kanto Gakuen Dai, Japan; Michelle Lee, Kaohsiung Hospitality
College, Taiwan; Stella Lee, Fooyin Universtiy, Taiwan; Shih-hao Lin,
Aletheia University, Taiwan; John Mancuso, Hitotsubashi University,
Japan; Michele Steele, Kyoai Gakuen, Takasaki Keizai, and Gunma Dai,
Japan; Chang-sup Sung, Dong-A University, Korea; Ki-wan Sung, Woosong
University, Korea; Hiroyo Yoshida, Toyo Daigaku Kogakubu, Japan.